# JAMAICAN

## Cocktails
## MIXED DRINKS

New Edition

## Mike Henry

© 1980 Mike Henry
First Edition 1980
Second Edition 1996
Revised Edition 2001
Revised Edition 2002
New Edition 2009
10 9 8 7 6 5 4 3 2 1

All LMH titles, imprints and distributed lines are available at special quantity discounts for bulk purchases for sales promotion, premiums, fund-raising, educational or institutional use.

Edited by Nicola Brown
Cover design by Sanya Dockery
Text layout and design by Sanya Dockery

Published by: LMH Publishing Limited
7 Norman Road,
LOJ Industrial Complex
Suite 10-11
Kingston C.S.O., Jamaica
Tel: 876-938-0005; 938-0712
Fax: 876-759-8752
Email: lmhbookpublishing@cwjamaica.com
Website: www.lmhpublishing.com

Printed in China                                    ISBN: 978-976-8202-31-4

# Acknowledgements

In this 'new' edition, as expected, there are new contributors and new bars discovered. And indeed new blends with a modern touch. I did not consult as much as I did in the past with Anthony Hogg's Cocktail and Mixed Drinks or Eddie Torado's book of the same title, all published by Hamlyn, nor did I refer as much to the Official Mixers Guide by Patrick Duffy and Robert Misch, as a lot of my imbibing was done in Jamaica (new wife kept me at home).

Suffice it to say that in staying home I really discovered the true creative ability of the Jamaican bartender as evidenced by the special recipes donated by Margaritaville, Strawberry Hill Hotel and Spa, Christopher's Jazz Café, SuperClubs and Sandals.

J. Wray and Nephew through Appleton and Sangster's were once again our staple and choice brand – we only choose the best, which undoubtedly includes Tia Maria. Red Stripe Beer, an old favourite, is now joined by Kingston Beer at our bar; and the dancehall crowd turned me on to Smirnoff Vodka (distributed by Diageo Jamaican Limited) and our 'visitor' Red Bull who in us found a new home. Dawn and I really fell for champagne and Red Bull on a balmy Miami South Beach night – true bliss.

*Happy Drinking* — see you in the mix.

*L. Michael Henry*

# Contents

# Introduction

In this the new millennium edition of Jamaican Cocktails, (Companion of Caribbean Cocktails) I have sought to individualize the editions of these two best selling titles.

Despite the passage of time, I have continued to follow my previous advice and cavort across Jamaica and the world, but this time hand in hand with my vibrant and vivacious wife, Dawn. And just as life does not stand still so have I seen the uniqueness of the Jamaican Cocktail unfold, as Jamaicans in their own way absorb the international brands and blend them to their own Jamaican taste and with their own touch of Jamaican class.

Thus I have seen Campari blended with White Overproof Rum to become 'Front end Lifter'; Guinness and Red Bull to become 'Liquid Viagra'; Rum and Cranberry to become 'Fast and Furious'; Appleton Rum, Crème de Banana and Rum Cream to become 'Dutty Whine', Champagne and Red Bull the 'Reggae Sun Riser' and Hennessy and Red Bull the 'Dancehall Craze'.

As the other alcohols, Vodka in particular, become more and more marketed; they are themselves blended with fruits and juices of Jamaica and made to become staples of a Jamaican bar.

Thus then the world has come to place Jamaican 'Watering Holes' among the top bars of the world, for who could visit Jamaica and fail to enjoy the marriage of nature all at its best. So let your imagination soar as it is stimulated by a sip of your favourite cocktail while you sit high atop Kingston at Strawberry Hill, or at Christophers Café in New Kingston while imbibing Brandy and Red Bull or sipping Jammin Reggae shot at Margaritaville on the hip strip of Montego Bay.

# Must Haves for a Jamaican Bar

The basic Jamaican bar should include white and dark rums, rum punch and Appleton rum, pimento liqueur and Sangster's World's End flavours of Sweet Ripe Banana, Rum and Raisin, Lychee, Island Coconut, Blue Mountain Coffee, and my favourite drink Campari.

To complete the bar, one must include scotch and rye whisky and bourbon, brandy, gin, vodka, vermouth (both sweet and dry), plus other basic liqueurs such as Advokaat, cherry brandy, Creme de Cacao, Creme de Menthe (both green and white) Cointreau, Drambuie, soft drinks and juices should include papaya and mango juice, pineapple juice, bitter lemon, cola, dry ginger ale, soda water, tonic water, orange juice, lemon juice, lime juice and tomato juice.

# Basic Bar Equipment

| | | |
|---|---|---|
| Cocktail Shaker or blender | Mixing glass and spoon | Cinnamon |
| Measures – ½ and 1 oz. | Ice bucket and tongs | Sugar |
| Corkscrew | Strainer | Salt |
| Openers (bottle and can) | Swizzle sticks | Cayenne |
| Coasters | Napkin | Nutmeg |
| Cloth for glasses | Grater | Oranges |
| Lemons | Cherries (maraschino) | Olives |
| Cocktail onions | Straws | Limes |
| Onions | Mint | Cucumber |
| Cloves | | |

# Tips for Making Good Drinks

- Always measure your ingredients. Don't guess!

- Stir all clear drinks. e.g. Martinis with ice.

- Blend in electric blender or shake well all drinks which contain fruit juices or cream. e.g. Whisky Sour or Brandy Alexander, to acquire a perfect blend.

- If possible serve all drinks in chilled glasses. Glasses may be chilled by placing them in the freezing compartment of your refrigerator for a few minutes or by placing a few cubes of ice in them prior to mixing the drink. Discard this ice before serving.

- Serve drinks ice cold. Have plenty of clean ice on hand. Put ice in glass, shaker or mixer first to chill quickly.

- Use fresh juices whenever possible.

- Use only the 'zest', the green part of the lemon/lime/orange when peel is requested. Do not include the 'pith' which is the white, bitter membrane of the rind.

- Always try to present a cocktail as attractively as possible.

- Drink the cocktail as soon as possible after mixing.

- Use clean, undamaged glasses.

- Add peel or cherry after the drink has been shaken or mixed.

- As a rule, shake hard to blend ingredients like fruit juices. Stir drinks made with clear liquors. For a 'frothy collar' on drinks, add a tablespoon of egg-white before shaking.

- In simple drinks, ice comes first then liquor, then mix. If a recipe uses sugar, it comes first. If carbonated beverages are being used they should be cold and added last. Always use freshly made ice for each round of drinks. Pre-chill glasses by filling with cracked ice. Store wet glasses in freezer to frost.

# Measurements

In Britain the smallest practical unit of liquid capacity is the fluid ounce (fl. oz.), in America it is a liquid ounce, and in Western Europe the centilitre (cl.).

| | | |
|---|---|---|
| Dessertspoon | = | ¼ fl. oz. |
| 6 out measure | = | 5/6 fl. oz. |
| 5 out measure | = | 1 fl. oz. |
| 4 out measure | = | 1¼ fl. oz. |
| Pony (USA) | = | 1 fl. oz (approx.) |
| Jigger (USA) | = | 1½ fl. oz (approx.) |

Cocktail glasses vary from 2/3½ oz. 2½ is an average UK size 4 oz. wine glasses (USA) is a good size for sours, like vodka and tomato juice.

A UK size is a 5 oz. wine glass

| | | | | |
|---|---|---|---|---|
| 14 cl | = | 5 fl oz | = | 1 gill or noggin |
| 23 cl | = | UK 8 oz wine glass | | |
| 28.4 cl. | = | 10 fl oz. | = | UK ½ pt. |
| 33 cl | = | 12 oz. wine glass | | |
| 55 cl | = | UK pint | | |
| 75 cl | = | One reputed qt. | = | usual wine bottle |
| 100 cl | = | 1 litre | | |

1.14 litre  =  40 fl. oz.  =  80 gills  =  1 Imperial Qt.  =  ¼ Imp. Gallon.

## Some Standard Bar Measures:

| | | |
|---|---|---|
| 1 dash | = | 1/6 teaspoon (1/32 ounce) |
| 1 teaspoon | = | 1/8 ounce |
| 1 tablespoon | = | 3/8 ounce |
| 1 Pony | = | 1 fl. oz. |
| 1 wine glass | = | 4 ounces |
| 1 split | = | 6 ounces |
| 1 cup | = | 8 ounces |

## Alcoholic Contents in Terms of Proof Spirit:

|  |  | Vol. % Alcohol added |
|---|---|---|
| Beer | 8.5% | 4.8 |
| Gin | 67% | 38.19 |
| Liqueurs | 52.7% | 30.03 |
| Rum | 60% | 39.33 |
| Whisky | 70% | 39.90 |
| Wine | 18.35% | 10.46 |

# Conversion Table

| To change from | To | Multiply by |
|---|---|---|
| grams | ounces | 0.035 |
| ounces | grams | 28.35 |
| kilograms | pounds | 2.205 |
| pounds | kilograms | 0.454 |
| centilitres | fluid ounces (U.K.) | 0.352 |
| centilitres | liquid ounces (U.S.A.) | 0.338 |
| gallons (U.K.) | litres | 4.50 |
| gallons (U.S.A.) | litres | 3.80 |
| litres | centilitres | 10.00 |

## Temperature:
°F to °C deduct 31 and multiply by 5/9.
°C to °F multiply by 9/5 and add 32.

# About Our Jamaican Rum

Rum had been known to China, Cyprus, and Sicily in Roman times, but the climate of the islands in the Caribbean was to make the West Indies the 'greatest producer' of this liquid gold.

On the British side of the world, rum was not known until Admirals Penn and Venables captured Jamaica in 1655, but it was known to the Europeans since the time Columbus discovered the island in 1494, and it was Columbus who actually brought cane cuttings to the W.I. from the Canaries.

Rum is a spirit that is distilled from molasses, which is the thick syrupy liquid that remains after the sugar is extracted from the juice of the sugar cane. In Jamaica it is either bottled without ageing or aged in oak casks for several years. In Jamaica the most famous brands are the Appleton Estate Jamaica Rum range of premium aged rums, which are all aged for several years and Wray & Nephew White Overproof Rum which is an unaged overproof rum.

The rum manufacturing process starts when the juice of the cane is extracted by crushing freshly cut cane. The juice is then clarified in large tanks to concentrate the sugar. This liquid is then crystallised and the sugar is extracted leaving a sugary molasses. The molasses is fermented by adding water and yeast, with the selection of yeast and the fermentation time governing the final character of the rum. After fermentation, the liquid is distilled using the traditional small batch copper pot distillation method that has been handed down since the inception of rum making in Jamaica, or the more modern column distillation method.

Rum is accepted as superior to Vodka, Whisky and Gin in the sense that since sugar is already present in the cane, there is no need for a preliminary malting process necessary to convert starch to sugar. Thus rum retains much more flavour.

Rum is the most versatile spirit in the world. It is capable of infinite variation in style, colour, age and body and there is a rum suited for every drinking occasion – from

fruit juices and cocktails to smooth sipping rums that are compared to the world's finest cognacs and scotches. Jamaican rum is also very good for hot drinks.

Often described as the Cognac of the Caribbean, the premium aged Jamaican rums are full flavoured, golden rums with complex flavours and a rich aroma.

The Appleton Estate Jamaica Rum range of premium aged rums range from the flagship brand, Appleton Estate V/X Jamaica Rum to the luxury brand Appleton Estate 21 Year Old Jamaica Rum, which is a blend of rums, each of which has been aged a minimum of 21 Years.

The local rum drink is 'Whites' — a strong clean overproof white rum consumed either straight or with any chaser from water through milk to coke. In its first distillation it is known as 'culu culu' and this is often times used locally to make rum punch of the strongest types.

# The Story of Rum

## FERMENTATION

Fermentation is the process whereby sugar is converted into Alcohol and Carbon Dioxide by the action of yeast. The main ingredient in the manufacturing of rum is molasses which is a by-product of the production of cane sugar. The molasses, containing about 60% sugar is mixed with water to bring the sugar content down to about 15%. The mixture is then pasteurized and pumped into the fermenting tanks. The fermentation of the sugar starts when a test tube of yeast is cultured in a sterile solution of molasses and water. Yeast is constantly multiplying so the culture is successively transferred to larger quantities of molasses and water (the mixture being called "live wash"), until it reaches the 2000 gallon "Bubb Tun" stage. By this time there are enough yeast cells to tackle the 24,000 gallons of live wash that has been pumped into one of the fermenters. There are approximately 26,000 lbs. of dissolved sugar in one of these fermenters and the original yeast culture, now many times multiplied is able to convert all this sugar into 3,000 gallons of rum and 13,000 lbs. $CO_2$ within a mere 30 hours. The bubbles and motion appearing on the surface of the fermenter are due entirely to the rapid movement of yeast and the $CO_2$ given off from its cells. When the sugar is used up the yeast dies from lack of nutrients and the mixture known as "dead wash' is now ready for distillation. About four, 24,000 gallon fermenters are distilled

each day so the mixing and fermentation process goes on 24 hours a day with a clock-like regularity. It is interesting to note that the wash is distilled about 5 days after the original test tube of yeast was cultured and at the end of the final phase there are about 150 lbs. of dead yeast cells left at the bottom of the fermenter. It takes about 1½ gallons of molasses to produce 1 gallon of rum.

# DISTILLATION

Rum is one of the purest alcoholic beverages because the fermentation takes place with sugar as the raw material, whereas, with some spirits, the starch in the grain has to be converted to sugar first before the fermenting process can begin. Distillation is the process whereby the alcohol in the dead wash is separated from the water (originally used to dilute the molasses) since alcohol boils at a lower temperature than water. The two methods of distilling used are the pot still and continuous still.

The Pot Still — is basically a kettle, which is used to contain the dead wash. Steam is applied to the kettle and the vapour given off is condensed and collected in three separate containers. The three products recovered are rum, (with an 85% alcohol content) high wine and low wine. The rum is put into storage tanks and the wines which have lower concentrations of alcohol are redistilled in the next cycle of the pot still. The pot still distillation method is the traditional method of distilling rum.

The Continuous Still — consists of three gigantic columns, each having a source of steam at their base. The first column is used for stripping the weak solution of alcohol from the wash, and the other two are used to purify and concentrate the alcoholic vapours. The columns consist of trays with perforations and down pipes that allow the liquid to flow from one tray to the next going down the column. The steam rises through the perforations and drives the alcohol vapours up the columns.

These vapours condense on the top trays and the liquid is drawn off the trays and cooled before going to the product tanks. The quality of the product depends on how high up the column the condensate is drawn off.

Thus, a mild rum product as well as the purest alcohol can be made on this still. The alcohol made is used in the manufacturing of gin, vodka and liqueurs while the mild rum which is light and dry is aged for future consumption.

# MATURATION AND BLENDING

Rum, when new, can be harsh to the taste so it must be aged for many years in 40 gallon oak casks. Oak is permeable so the rum breathes and air passing through the pores of the wood, mellows the rum and alters the taste. At the same time the rum takes on some colour from the oak. On walking through a warehouse one will notice

the pleasant smell and temperature in the building. This is caused by evaporation of the rum vapour through the pores of the wood which in itself has a cooling effect. There are losses during the process of aging but nothing has ever been found to replace this system of producing a mellow, smooth product.

Once the rum has been aged the contents of each cask are carefully tested by experienced blenders and then mixed in vats where the process of "marrying the blends" takes place. The "marrying" process allows the different rums in the blend to fuse together and this results in a more rounded product. Brands of rum are derived from varying mixtures of pot still and continuous still products, the former gives the rum its character and the latter the lightness. The dark "Punch-style" rums are made by the addition of caramel and some aged rums are filtered through activated charcoal to remove the colour and thus you have aged white rums also.

The blended rums are then reduced in strength by the addition of purified water and after filtering and polishing they are bottled in the most modern filling machines.

## WHITE RUM:

Jamaica boasts two distinct styles of white rum. White rum can either be an overproof unaged spirit such as Wray & Nephew White Overproof Rum or an aged spirit such as Appleton Genesis. Although both are very different in terms of flavour and character, both are excellent for mixing.

Wray & Nephew White Overproof Rum adds a unique rum character to drinks and is the secret ingredient in many signature cocktails.

Appleton Genesis is a light, smooth rum that imparts a subtle taste and delicate aroma in all drinks in which it is served.

## APPLETON SPECIAL:

Appleton Special Jamaica Rum was first introduced during the Second World War as an alternative to Whisky, which was in short supply. This smooth, fragrant rum, proved to be extremely popular with Jamaicans and is still a favourite today where it is enjoyed with traditional Jamaican chasers such as cola, ginger ale and soda water or in cocktails.

# Liqueurs

## Sangster's Jamaica Original Rum Cream

High in the Blue Mountains of Jamaica are created some of the finest liqueurs in the world. Pioneered by the late Dr. Ian Sangster, a Scotsman who migrated to Jamaica in 1967 (the brand is now owned by Lascelles deMercado & Company Limited), Sangster's Jamaica Original Rum Cream captures the taste of Jamaica with its delightful aroma and exotic flavour. These liqueurs are blended from selected aged Jamaican rums and a range of exotic fruits and spices. The warm spirited heart of these liqueurs is a balanced blend of carefully selected aged Jamaican rums.

Lovingly produced in the cool tropical climate, these liqueurs have gained gold medals at international wine and spirits contests in London (1976) and Bristol (1978) and most recently one from Monde Quality Select Awards. They serve as superb after-dinner drinks or provide the basis of a number of intriguing mixed drinks. Sangster's Jamaica Coffee Liqueur is the finest of Caribbean Coffee Liqueurs.

## Sangster's Coffee Rum Liqueur

This world-renowned liqueur with Jamaican Rum base is one of the rewarding things about a visit to the Caribbean. Try it with a measure of cognac and champagne and garnish with a black cherry.

# Tia Maria
## THE LEGEND OF TIA MARIA

The original recipe of Tia Maria dates back to the seventeenth century during the Colonial Wars when the English invaded the Spanish colony of Jamaica. It is said that during the hasty flight by the Spaniards, a beautiful young girl of Spanish nobility was separated from her parents and was left with only her maid, Maria, who had managed to rescue some of the family's most valued possessions. Among these was a small treasure box containing a manuscript with a secret family recipe written on it.

Later, the girl married and had a big family with an officer of the British forces. On the wedding day of their eldest daughter, she passed on the small treasure box to her daughter, a tradition that would be followed many years to come. In honour of her dedicated maid, she named the liqueur Tia Maria.

However, as time passed the legend seemed to have been forgotten and the treasure box lost until the latter was rediscovered by Dr. Kenneth Leigh Evans. He used the recipe and introduced the world to this famous flavourful Coffee Liqueur, made from sugar cane and coffee. One favourite way to serve it is with milk over ice and a dash of nutmeg.

## WISHFUL THINKING

An obese Jamaican woman at a party walked up to a man and told him, "If yuh were my husband, mi would poison yuh drink."

The man replied, "If you were my wife, mi would drink it."

## FOOD FOR THOUGHT

A man walks out of a bar totally hammered, only to be greeted by a snobby woman. She takes one look at him.

"You, sir, are drunk!"

"And you ma'am, are ugly. But when I wake up, I will be sober!"

## ANIMAL FARM

A lady goes into a bar with her goose. The bartender comes up to her and says, "Why did you have to bring the pig in here with you?"

The lady responded airily, "Excuse me, I think this is a goose."

The bartender replies, "Excuse me, I was talking to the goose."

# Rum Based Drinks

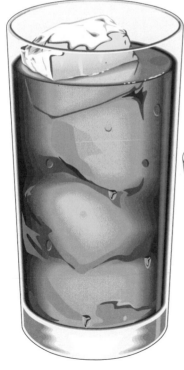

Mac made his way along the office corridor. He looked intently at the letters on the door and with narrowed eyes turned the handle and walked in.

'Ist thish Alcoholicks Anonymush? He lisped.

'Yes, sir! D'you wish to join?'

'No, tae resign.'

# Some Favourite Rum Drinks

## BANANA DAIQUIRI

1½ oz. rum
1 tablespoon Curacao
1½ oz. lime juice

1 teaspoon sugar
1 sliced medium-sized banana
1 cup crushed ice

- Combine ingredients in a blender and blend at low speed for five seconds.
- Then blend at high speed until firm.
- Pour into champagne glass. Top with a cherry.

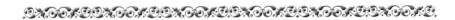

## BIG BAMBOO

2 oz. Jamaican Rum
¼ oz. lime juice
¼ oz. grenadine

¼ oz. Triple Sec
1 oz. orange juice

- Shake, pack a large mug or tall glass with powdered ice and pour mixture over same.
- Garnish with a sprig of mint and serve with a straw.

## BLACK ROSE

A jigger of rum
Cold black coffee

1 teaspoon sugar

- Add ice in a tall glass, stir and serve.

# BLOODY MARY

2 oz. Caribbean White Rum
4 ¼ oz. tomato juice
¼ oz. lime juice

3 or 4 dash Worcestershire Sauce
3 or 4 drops Tabasco Sauce
Salt

- Stir with cracked ice. Strain and serve.

# BUCCANEER PUNCH

3 oz. Caribbean Special Rum
1 oz. lime juice
3 teaspoons sugar

Dash of Angostura Bitters
1 cup cracked ice

- Shake and pour unstrained into glass, adding a slice of lime and a little nutmeg.
- Serve with a straw. For tall drinks, top up with soda water.

# CARNIVAL JUMP-UP

2 oz. dark rum
½ oz. grenadine syrup
½ oz. fresh lime juice

1 oz. fresh coconut cream
Slice of pineapple
Slice of lime

- Shake all liquids and pour into a small Bengali glass.
- Garnish with pineapple and lime. Serves 6.

# COCONUT OAK

1¼ oz. dark rum
½ oz. gin
½ oz. Carypton

2 oz. coconut water/milk
½ oz. syrup
½ oz. fresh lime juice

- Shake all ingredients with crushed ice.
- Serve in a coconut shell with straws. Serves 6.

3

# CREOLE COCKTAIL

1 oz. amber rum
1 oz. dark rum
½ oz. orange juice
½ oz. syrup
1 cherry

½ oz. Carypton
2 dash grenadine syrup
1 dash fresh coconut cream
Sprig of mint
Slice of lime

- Shake all liquids with crushed ice, then strain into a tall glass.
- Garnish with mint, the slice of lime and cherry.

# DAWN'S SURPRISE

1½ oz. rum
Juice from 1 lime
3 teaspoons powdered sugar

1 oz. grapefruit juice
1 dash bitters

- Shake with ice and strain into cocktail glass.

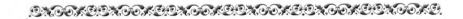

# DIP-AN-FALL-BACK

2 oz. light rum
½ teaspoon Curacao
1 teaspoon orange juice

1 teaspoon lemon juice
1 teaspoon raspberry syrup

- Shake with ice and strain into cocktail glass.
- Decorate with small slice of pineapple.

# EL PRESIDENTE

I jigger light rum
1/3 jigger Curacao

1/3 jigger dry vermouth
I dash grenadine

- Shake well with ice and strain into cocktail glass.

# FROZEN DAIQUIRI (STELLA'S JOY)

Crush two cups ice in a blender. Add four jiggers of light rum.

I tablespoon fresh lime juice                    2 tablespoons powdered sugar
Blend in by preference either:
½ of a very ripe banana or 1/3 cup canned mango fruit or pineapple chunks

- The final consistency should be like snow (whatever the flavour chosen).
- Serve in a stemmed 4 oz wine glass with a straw and topped with a maraschino cherry.

# GREEN PARROT

I oz. Wray & Nephew White Overproof Rum        4 oz. orange juice
I oz. Blue Curacao

- Pour ingredients one at a time, in the order listed above, into a large stemmed glass over ice. Do not mix. Garnish with an orange slice.

# HIGHWIND

2 oz. Appleton Jam Rum
I oz. pineapple juice
½ oz. lime juice

I oz. grenadine syrup
½ oz. orange juice

- Shake and serve with ice and a slice of orange.

GREEN PARROT (page 5)

# HURRICANE

1 oz. dark rum
1 tablespoon passion fruit syrup

1 oz. light rum
2 teaspoons lime juice

- Shake with ice and strain into cocktail glass.

# KINGSTON NO.1

½ oz. rum
¼ Kummel

¼ orange juice
1 dash pimento dram

- Shake with ice and strain into glass.

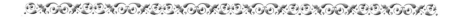

# KIN-PUPPA-LICK

1½ oz. Rum Menthe
1½ oz. Creme de Menthe (white)

1 dash lemon juice

- Shake with ice and strain into cocktail glass.

# LIMBO

1½ oz. dark rum
½ teaspoonCréme de Menthe
½ teaspoon Triple Sec Curacao

1 tablespoon lime juice
1 teaspoon powdered sugar

- Shake with ice and strain into cocktail glass.  Add lime slice.

## MAI-TAI

2 oz. light rum
I tablespoon lime juice
I tablespoon Orgeat or almond-flavoured syrup

I oz. Curacao
I tablespoon grenadine
½ teaspoon powdered sugar.

- Shake with ice and strain into a large old-fashioned glass about 1/3 full with crushed ice.
- Decorate with maraschino cherry speared to wedge of fruit, preferably fresh pineapple.
- For a 'hair raiser', top with a dash of 100% proof rum and for a real Caribbean/ Hawaiian effect, float an orchid on each drink. Serve with straws.

## MORNING ROSE

½ jigger light rum
¼ jigger Curacao

1/3 jigger grenadine
1/3 jigger lemon juice

- Shake well with ice and strain into cocktail glass.

## NAKED LADY

½ light rum
½ sweet vermouth
4 dash apricot brandy

2 dash grenadine
4 dash lemon juice

- Shake well with ice and strain into cocktail glass.

## NATIONAL

1I/3 jiggers light rum
1/3 jigger pineapple juice

1/3 jigger apricot brandy
I cherry

- Shake well with shaved ice and strain into glass.
- Serve with pineapple stick or wedge and cherry.

## OLYMPIA

1 jigger dark rum                              Juice of ½ lime
2/3 jigger cherry brandy

* Shake well with ice and strain into cocktail glass.

## ORANGE DAIQUIRI

1 ½ oz. Appleton Special Jamaica Rum          Juice of 1 orange
Juice of ¼ lime                               1 oz sugar syrup
1 scoop crushed ice

* Mix all ingredients in blender, serve in a cocktail glass and garnish with orange slice.

## PASSION DAIQUIRI

1½ oz. rum                                     1 teaspoon powdered sugar
1 tablespoon passion fruit juice              Juice 1 lime

* Shake with ice and strain into cocktail glass.

## PINA COLADA

3 oz. rum                                      3 tablespoons coconut milk
3 tablespoons crushed pineapple

* Place in blender with two cups of crushed ice and blend at high speed for a short time.
* Strain into collins glass and serve with straw.

**ORANGE DAIQUIRI** (page 9)

## PINEAPPLE COCKTAIL

1½ oz. rum                              ¾ oz. pineapple juice
½ teaspoon lemon juice

* Shake with ice and strain into cocktail glass.

## PINEAPPLE FIZZ

1 oz. rum                               1 teaspoon grenadine
1 tablespoon lime juice                 1 teaspoon sweet cream

* Shake with ice and strain into cocktail glass.
* Add a black cherry soaked in rum.

## PIRATE'S PUNCH

2 parts dark rum                        1 dash Angostura Bitters
1 part sweet vermouth

* Stir well with ice and strain into glass.

## PLANTERS COCKTAIL

1½ oz. Jamaican Rum                     ½ teaspoon powdered sugar
Juice of 1 lemon

* Shake with ice and strain into cocktail glass.

## PLANTERS PUNCH

3 parts Jamaican rum
3 parts water including ice or soda
A dash of Curacao or Angostura (optional)

I part lime juice
2 parts sugar syrup

- Serve in tall glass with cherries and orange slices.
- Each Caribbean island makes this drink with its own native rum.

## PORT ROYAL

I pt. Jamaican rum
I teaspoon lime juice

I pt. Sangster's Coffee Liqueur

- Serve over ice, sip and listen for the sunken Port Royal Church bells to ring.

## PUNCH-A-CREME

6 oz. white rum
3 oz. dark rum
I egg

6 oz. condensed milk
6 oz. evaporated milk

- Whisk all ingredients together.
- Serve in short glasses over ice cubes. Serves 6.

## ROLLING CALF

1 ½ oz. Wray & Nephew White Overproof Rum over ice topped with Red Bull.

## RUM & COCONUT WATER

- I oz. rum over ice topped with fresh coconut water.

## RUM & COKE

- I oz. rum over ice topped with Coke in a highball glass.
- Add a squeeze of lime or lemon.

## RUM & GINGER ALE

- I oz. rum over ice topped with ginger ale.

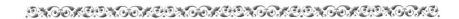

## RUM & TONIC

- I½ oz. white rum over ice cubes in a highball glass.
- Fill with tonic water and add a squeeze of lime or lemon.

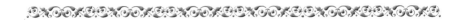

## RUM & WATER

- I½ oz. rum over ice cubes in an old-fashioned glass topped with plain water.

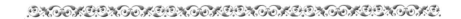

## RUM DAIQUIRI

| | |
|---|---|
| 2 ½ oz. Wray & Nephew White Overproof Rum | 2 level teaspoons sugar |
| ¼ oz. lime juice | 3 to 4 ice cubes |

- Shake and strain contents into a cocktail glass.

## RUM DAISY

Whereas crustas are served cold, the ice remaining behind in the shaker, daisies are 'On the Rocks' drinks with raspberry syrup. Lemon juice and fruit being added to the spirit chosen.

Fill a goblet with ice.

Put in a shaker
1½ oz. rum                                    ¾ oz. raspberry syrup
the juice of ½ lemon

- Shake and strain into goblet. Add soda and garnish with fruit.

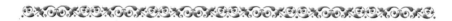

## RUM SCREWDRIVER

1½ oz.  Wray & Nephew White Overproof Rum      A pinch of sugar (optional)
3 or 4 ice cubes                               3 oz. orange juice

- Place ice cubes and rum into a highball glass and top up with orange juice.

## SANTIAGO

2 jiggers Bacardi Rum                          4 dash lime juice
2 dash grenadine

- Stir well with ice and strain into glass.

## SHARK'S TOOTH

1 jigger light rum                             ½ jigger lime juice
½ jigger 151 proof rum                         Dash sugar syrup
½ jigger lemon juice                           Dash grenadine

- Pour into large glass with ice. Top with soda.

## SPANISH TOWN

1 jigger medium rum                              2 dash Curacao

- Shake with shaved ice and strain into glass. Serve with a grating of nutmeg.

## ST. MARY CHAMPAGNE

½ teaspoon rum                                   ½ teaspoon Créme de Banana
Chilled Champagne

- Pour rum and banana liqueur into champagne glass.
- Fill with champagne and stir lightly.
- Add a slice of banana.

## WATERMELON MARTINI

1 ½ oz. Appleton Jamaica Rum                      2 cups cubed watermelon flesh
¾ oz. Sugar syrup

- Crush watermelon in the bottom of a shaker.
- Add other ingredients; shake with ice and strain into a martini glass.
- Garnish with Watermelon Wedge.

## WHITE RUM & SORREL LIQUEUR

To make sorrel, pour boiling water over ½ lb. sorrel flowers from which the petals have been removed. Cool, strain and sweeten to taste. Mix this with one pint Wray and Nephew White Overproof Rum and let it stand for a few days. Add Jamaican ginger to taste and drink as an after dinner liqueur.

WATERMELON MARTINI (page 15)

# YELLOW BIRD

1½ oz. rum
¼ oz. orange juice
Dash of Galliano

3 ozs. pineapple juice
¾ oz. Crème de Banana
¼ oz. apricot brandy

- Shake well and serve in tall glass.

# Appleton Estate Jamaica Rum

The Appleton Estate Jamaica Rum range is the pride of Jamaica. This range of premium aged rums is produced on the Appleton Estate in the Nassau Valley in St. Elizabeth. The Appleton Estate is the oldest sugar estate and distillery in Jamaica in continuous production, with the first known documentation of rum production on the Estate being dated 1749.

The brands that make up the Appleton Estate Jamaica Rum range include the flagship brand, Appleton Estate V/X Jamaica Rum, the super premium Appleton Estate Reserve Jamaica Rum, the ultra premium Appleton Estate Extra 12 Year Old Jamaica Rum, and the luxury rums, Appleton Estate Master Blenders' Legacy and Appleton Estate 21 Year Old Jamaica Rum. The company will also release a Limited Edition 30 Year Old Rum, Appleton Estate 30 Year Old Jamaica Rum, of which only 1,440 bottles will be produced during the second half of 2008.

The Appleton Estate Jamaica Rum has been awarded numerous gold medals, trophies and accolades in international competitions. It is the leading imported premium aged rum in a number of countries including Canada, Mexico, Peru and New Zealand.

## JOY'S PASSION

1 ½ oz. Appleton Estate V/X Jamaica Rum  
2 oz. mango nectar  
Juice of ¼ lime  

½ oz. peach schnapps  
½ oz. clear syrup  

- Combine ingredients in a shaker with ice and mix well.
- Serve in a martini glass and garnish with a lime wedge.

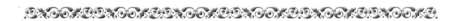

## JOY'S STRAWBERRY SENSATION

1 ½ oz. Appleton V/X  
Fresh strawberries or strawberry puree  
1 tsp. lime juice  

¾ Cointreau  
1 oz. orange juice  

- Stir all ingredients in a shaker with 2 scoops of ice and shake for 10 seconds.
- Serve in a margarita glass and garnish with a fresh strawberry and lime wedge.

**JOY'S PASSION** (page 18)

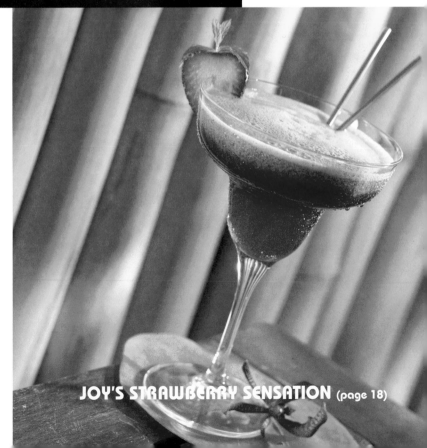

**JOY'S STRAWBERRY SENSATION** (page 18)

GINGH GINNAL (page 21)

DUTTY WHINE (page 21

FAST AND FURIOUS (page 21)

YOUNG AND RESTLESS (page

# *Appleton's Attitude Cocktails*

## DUTTY WHINE

1 ¼ oz. Appleton Jamaica Rum
1 oz. rum
1 oz. coconut cream

¼ oz. Crème de Banana
1 oz. Tia Maria
½ fresh banana

- Blend all ingredients and serve in a highball glass.  Garnish with a banana slice.

## FAST AND FURIOUS

1 ½ oz. Appleton Jamaica Rum

2 oz. cranberry juice

- Combine ingredients in a shaker filled with ice and mix well. Serve in a martini glass.

## GINGER GINNAL

1 oz. Appleton Jamaica Rum

2 oz. ginger ale

- Combine ingredients in a shaker and serve.
- Garnish with a lemon wedge.

## YOUNG AND RESTLESS

Juice of half a lime
1 oz. Appleton Jamaica Rum

1 oz. Genesis
Maraschino cherry for garnish

- Combine ingredients in a shaker and serve. Garnish with Maraschino cherry.

# Gin Based Drinks

Then there was Rafferty's attempt to drown his troubles in drink. He found they could swim…

# ALLEN SPECIAL

2/3 part dry gin
1/3 part Maraschino

1 dash lemon juice

- Stir well with ice and strain into glass.

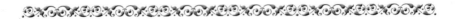

# ATTA BOY

2/3 part dry gin
1/3 part dry vermouth

4 dash grenadine

- Stir well with ice and strain into glass. Serve with a twist of lemon peel.

# CREOLE COCKTAIL

1½ oz. dry gin
1 egg white

1 dash orange bitters
½ teaspoon grenadine

- Shake with ice and strain into cocktail glass.

# DEEP SEA

½ part Old Tom Gin
½ part dry vermouth

1 dash Pernod
1 dash orange bitters

- Stir well with ice and strain into glass. Squeeze lemon peel over top and serve with an olive.

# GIBSON

- Mix a Martini and serve with two pearl onions, in place of lemon peel or olive.

## GIMLET

2 measures gin

1 lime juice cordial

- Shake well with ice and strain. Add soda water if required.

## GIN & IT

Unshaken:
- Combine 1 part sweet vermouth in a cocktail glass with 1 part gin. Add a cherry.

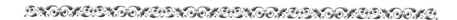

## GIN & TONIC

- Add large measure of gin to tumbler containing ice, fill with chilled tonic water and add a slice of lemon or lime.

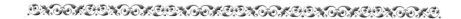

## GIN TROPICAL

1 oz. gin
1 oz. passion fruit syrup
½ oz. Blue Curacao

Soda water
Maraschino cherry
Slice of orange

- Shake gin, syrup and Curacao.
- Strain into glass and top with soda water.
- Serve with drinking straw, cherry and slice of orange for garnish.

## GOLDEN SUN FIZZ

Large measure of gin
Juice of 1 lemon

1 teaspoon sugar
1 egg yolk

- Shake well with ice and pour into tumbler containing ice, and fill with soda water.

## GRAPEFRUIT COCKTAIL

1 oz. grapefruit juice
1 teaspoon Maraschino

1 oz. dry gin

- Shake with ice and strain into cocktail glass. Serve with a cherry.

## IMPERIAL COCKTAIL

1½ oz. dry vermouth
½ teaspoon Maraschino (a cherry liqueur)

1¼ oz. dry gin
1 dash bitters

- Stir with ice and strain into cocktail glass. Serve with a cherry.

## J.O.S

1/3 part dry gin
1/3 part dry vermouth
1/3 part sweet vermouth

1 dash brandy
1 dash orange bitters
1 dash lemon or lime juice

- Stir well with ice and strain into glass.
- Twist lemon peel over top.

## JAMAICA GLOW COCKTAIL

1 oz. dry gin
1 tablespoon Claret

1 tablespoon orange juice
1 teaspoon Appleton Rum

- Shake and strain (with ice) into cocktail glass.

# JOHN COLLINS

Large measure of gin                    I teaspoon sugar
Juice of I lemon

- Pour into tumbler containing ice cubes and fill up with soda water.
- Add a dash of Angostura Bitters, stir and serve with a slice of lemon.

# MARTINI

- The proportions used in this famous cocktail can be varied to taste, the proportion of gin to dry vermouth should never be less than 4 to I, but may be as high as I0 to I. These ingredients should be put into an ice-cold mixing glass, stirred with ice, and then strained.
- An olive or lemon peel can be added according to taste.

# MARTINI - DRY

I part gin                              I part dry vermouth
I dash orange bitters

- Mix I part gin with I part dry vermouth and add a dash of orange bitters (optional). Squeeze zest of lemon peel over the cocktail and optionally add an olive.

# MARTINI - MEDIUM

4 parts gin                             I part dry vermouth
I part sweet vermouth

- Mix 4 parts gin with I part dry vermouth and I part sweet vermouth

# MARTINI - SWEET

2 parts gin                                    I part sweet vermouth

- Mix 2 parts gin with I part sweet vermouth and add a cherry.

# MAYFAIR

I measure gin                                  I juiced orange
3 dash apricot brandy

- Shake with ice and strain.

# MOONSHINE

¼ part dry gin                                 ¼ Maraschino
¼ part dry vermouth                            I- 2 drops Pernod

- Shake well with ice and strain into glass.

# NEGRONI

I measure gin                                  I part sweet vermouth
I part Campari

- Place ingredients into a tall glass with ice.
- Add a slice of orange and serve.

# OPERA

2/3 part dry gin                               I/6 part Maraschino
I/6 part Dubonnet

- Stir well with ice and strain into glass.
- Squeeze orange peel over top.

## ORANGE BLOSSOM

I measure gin                           I juiced orange

- Shake well with ice and strain.
- A dash of grenadine can be added to taste.

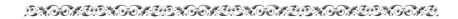

## PAPAYA SLING

I½ oz. dry gin                          Juice of I lime
I dash bitters                          I tablespoon papaya syrup

- Shake with ice and strain into collins glass over ice cubes.
- Fill with carbonated water and stir.
- Add a pineapple stick.

## PARADISE

I/3 part dry gin                        I/3 part apricot brandy
I/3 part orange or lemon juice

- Stir well with ice and strain

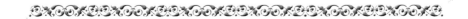

## PERFECT COCKTAIL

I½ oz. dry gin                          ¾ oz. dry vermouth
¾ oz. sweet vermouth

- Stir gin, dry and sweet vermouth. Serve in 3 oz. cocktail glass.

# PINK GIN

I measure gin                                                         water to taste

- Roll two dash of Angostura Bitters round a glass, add a large measure of gin and water to taste.

# POLO NO. 1

1/3 part dry gin                                                      1/3 sweet vermouth
1/3 part dry vermouth                                                Juice of 1/3 lime

- Shake well with ice and strain into glass.

# QUEEN ELIZABETH

½ part dry gin                                                        ¼ part lemon juice
¼ part Cointreau                                                     I dash Pernod

- Stir well with ice and strain into glass.

# QUEENIE'S COCKTAIL

I part dry gin                                                        I part pineapple juice
I part dry vermouth                                                  I maraschino cherry
I piece pineapple for decoration                                     I part sweet vermouth

- Shake gin, dry and sweet vermouth and pineapple juice.
- Serve in cocktail glass with pineapple and cherry.

## ROYAL SMILE

½ part dry gin
½ part grenadine

2 dash lemon juice

- Stir well with ice and strain into glass.

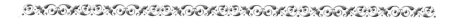

## SATAN'S WHISKERS

I part gin
I part Grand Marnier
I part dry vermouth

I part sweet vermouth
I part orange juice

- Shake together and add a dash of orange bitters.

## SOUTH SIDE

2 jiggers dry gin
Juice of ½ lemon

½ tablespoon powdered sugar
2 sprigs of fresh mint

- Shake well with ice and strain into glass.
- Add a dash of soda water if desired.

## TANGO

2 parts gin
I part sweet vermouth

I part dry vermouth
2 dash Orange Curacao

- Shake together and add a dash of orange juice.

## TRINITY

1/3 part dry gin
1/3 part dry vermouth

1/3 part sweet vermouth

* Stir well with ice and strain into glass.

## WHITE CARGO

½ part dry gin

½ part vanilla ice cream

* No ice is necessary. Shake together till blended and pour into glass.

## WHITE WITCH

2 measures gin
1 part lemon juice

1 part Cointreau

* Shake with ice and strain.

For further reference on White Witch read Mike Henry's **Rosehall's White Witch: The Legend of Annie Palmer.**

## YELLOW DAISY

* Mix 2 parts gin with 1 part dry vermouth and 1 part Grand Marnier.

## COINCIDENCES

A man stumbles up to the only other patron in a bar and asks if he could buy him a drink. "Why of course," was the reply.

The first man then asks: "Where are you from?"

"I'm from Kingston," replies the second man.

The first man responds: "You don't say! I'm from Kingston too! Let's have another round to Kingston."

"Of course," replies the second man.

"I'm curious," the first man then asks: "Where in Kingston are you from?"

"Barbican," was the reply.

"I can't believe it," says the first man. "I'm from Barbican too! Let's have another drink to Barbican."

"Of course," replies the second man.

Curiosity again strikes and the first man asks: "What school did you go to?"

"Kingston College," replies the second man, "I graduated in '72."

"This is unbelievable!" the first man says. "I went to Kingston College and I graduated in '72, too!"

About that time in comes one of the regulars and sits down at the bar. "What's been going on?" he asks the bartender.

"Nothing much," replies the bartender. "The Brady twins are drunk again."

# Vodka Based Drinks

*Prayer of a Catholic girl...*

*'Oh Virgin Mother, who didst conceive without sinning, teach me how to sin without conceiving.'*

# Smirnoff Vodka

Smirnoff Vodka is one of the world's most popular and best selling vodkas. It became extremely popular in Jamaica in the early 2000 with the introduction of Smirnoff Ice, now available in Red and Black. It is the drink of choice for many party going fanatics.

# Smirnoff Signature Drink Options

## COSMOPOLITAN

1½ oz. Smirnoff No. 21 Vodka
1 oz. OceanSpray Cranberry Juice

½ oz. Triple Sec
1 Lemon Wheel

- Full cocktail shaker with 1 ½ cups cracked ice.
- Add all ingredients except the lime wedge.
- Shake vigorously to blend and chill.
- Strain mixture into martini glass.
- Lightly squeeze lime wedge over drink and drop into glass to garnish.

## SMIRNOFF CITRUS WITH A TWIST

1 oz. Smirnoff Citrus Flavoured Vodka

3 oz. Tonic or Soda

- Serve over ice in a highball glass.
- Garnish with a lemon twist.

COSMOPOLITAN (page 36)

**SMIRNOFF CITRUS WITH A TWIST** (page 36)

## SMIRNOFF GREEN APPLE VODKA & LEMON-LIME SODA

1½ oz. Smirnoff Green Apple Vodka  
1 Wedge lemon

3 oz. Lemon-lime soda

- Fill glass with ice.
- Add Smirnoff Green Apple Vodka and lemon-lime soda.
- Stir well and garnish with lemon.

## SMIRNOFF VANILLLA VODKA & COLA

1½ oz. Smirnoff Vanillla Vodka  
1 Wedge lime

3 oz. Cola

- Fill glass with ice.
- Add Smirnoff Vanilla Vodka and cola.
- Stir well and garnish with lime.

**SMIRNOFF GREEN APPLE VODKA & LEMON-LIME SODA** (page 39)

**SMIRNOFF VANILLLA VODKA & COLA** (page 39)

# Smirnoff Black No. 55 Vodka

## DOUBLE BLACK MARTINI

$1\frac{3}{4}$ oz. Smirnoff Black

$\frac{1}{5}$ oz. Johnnie Walker Black

- Coat martini glass with Johnnie Walker Black.
- Stir Smirnoff Black in mixing glass with ice.
- Strain into martini glass.
- Lemon twist opitonal.

## FRESH 55

$1\frac{3}{4}$ Smirnoff Black
3 lemon wedges
1 oz. ginger ale

1 sugar cube
2 sprigs of mint

- Add sugar cube, lemon and sprig of mint to mixing glass and muddle.
- Add Smirnoff Black and shake with ice.
- Strain into a highball glass filled with ice.
- Top with ginger ale and garnish with a sprig of mint.

**DOUBLE BLACK MARTINI** (page 42)

**FRESH 55** (page 42)

# AIR CONDITIONER

2 oz. vodka                          1 oz. Cointreau

- Low-calorie coke to taste. Serve on the rocks.

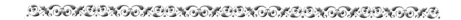

# AQUEDUCT

1½ oz. vodka                         1½ teaspoons apricot brandy
1 ¾ teaspoons Curacao                1 tablespoon lime juice

- Combine and shake all ingredients and strain into cocktail glass.
- Add a twist of orange peel.

# BANANA PUNCH

2 oz. Smirnoff Vodka                 1½ teaspoons apricot brandy
Juice of ½ lime

- Pour into collins glass filled with crushed ice.
- Add tonic water and top with slices of banana and sprigs of mint.

# BARBARA (RUSSIAN BEAR)

1/3 part vodka                       1/3 part Créme de Cacao
1/3 part cream

- Stir well with ice and strain into glass.

# BLACK RUSSIAN

1½ oz. Smirnoff Vodka
¾ oz. Tia Maria or Sangster's World's End Blue Mountain Coffee Liqueur

- Pour over ice cubes in old-fashioned cocktail glass.

# BLENHEIM

- Shake together 2 parts vodka, 1 part Tia Maria and 1 part fresh orange juice.

# BLOODY MARY

2 oz. vodka
2 drops Tabasco sauce
1 dash Worcestershire sauce
3 cubes ice

¼ oz. lemon juice
tomato juice
Salt and pepper

- In 10 oz. glass, put Worcestershire sauce, Tabasco sauce and lemon juice.
- Add salt and pepper. Mix together and then add ice cubes and vodka and top with tomato juice.
- Serve with swizzle stick.

# BULL FROG

1½ oz. vodka

4 oz. limeade

- Pour vodka into tall glass with ice. Fill with limeade and stir.

## BULL SHOT

Vigorously shake together:

1 oz. vodka
2 oz. tomato juice

2 oz. condensed consomme

* Add a dash of Worcestershire sauce, Tabasco, cayenne and celery salt.

## EGGHEAD

1½ oz. vodka
4 oz. orange juice

1 egg in a blender

* Mix and pour into a tall glass with ice.

## GODMOTHER

1 jigger of vodka

1 jigger Amaretto di Saronno

* Stir with cracked ice.

## HARVEY WALLBANGER

1 jigger (1½ oz.) vodka
½ jigger Galliano

3 jiggers orange juice

* Pour vodka in a tall glass filled with ice cubes, pour orange juice and float Galliano on top.

# ICE PICK

1½ oz. vodka                    Lemon-flavoured iced tea

- Pour vodka into a tall glass with ice.
- Top up with iced tea and stir.

# JUNGLE JIM

1 oz. vodka                     1 oz. Creme de Banana
1 oz. milk

- Pour into a short glass with ice and stir.

# KANGAROO

1 jigger vodka                  ½ jigger dry vermouth

- Serve with cracked ice and strain into glass.
- Serve with a twist of lemon peel.

# MOSCOW MULE

2 oz. vodka                     Ginger Beer
1 oz. lemon juice               Mint for decoration
3 cubes ice

- Put 3 cubes ice in a 10 oz. glass, add vodka and lemon juice and fill with ginger beer.
- Decorate with mint and serve.

# ROAD RUNNER

1 oz. vodka                                    ½ oz. Amaretto di Saronno
½ oz. coconut cream

- Mix in blender with ½ scoop of crushed ice for 15 seconds.
- Rim edge of chilled 4 ½ oz. champagne glass with a slice of orange.
- Dip rim in sugar and nutmeg mixture.
- Pour cocktail into prepared glass and top with dash of nutmeg.

# RUSSIAN

1 jigger vodka                                 1 jigger Créme de Cacao
1 jigger dry gin

- Stir well with ice and strain into glass.

# SALTY DOG

1½ oz. vodka                                   5 oz. grapefruit juice
¼ teaspoon salt.

- Pour into highball glass over ice cubes. Stir well.

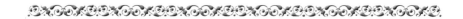

# SCREWDRIVER

1½ oz. vodka                                   Slice of orange
3 cubes ice                                    1 maraschino cherry
Orange juice

- Place ice cubes and vodka into a 10 oz. high ball glass and top up with orange juice.
- Garnish with slice of orange and cherry and serve.

# SEA URCHIN

1½ oz. vodka                                    Grapefruit juice

- Serve in a 10 oz. highball glass with ice. Top up with grapefruit juice.

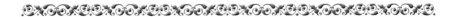

# SUN STROKE

3 oz. grapefruit juice (unsweetened)            1½ oz. vodka
Add Triple Sec or Cointreau

- Stir together in a short glass filled with ice.

# THE MACHETE

1½ oz. vodka                                    2/3 glass pineapple juice

- Pour into a tall glass with ice. Stir.

# VODKA MIST

1½ oz. vodka                                    Twist of lemon

- Pour vodka in a cocktail shaker and add a twist of lemon.
- Serve unstrained in old-fashioned glass.

# VODKA-ON-THE-ROCKS

1½ oz. vodka                                    3 cubes ice

- Pour vodka over ice cubes in old-fashioned glass and serve.

## VODKA SOUR

2 oz. vodka                                    ½ teaspoon powdered sugar
Juice ½ lemon

- Shake with ice and strain into sour glass.
- Decorate with half-slice of lemon and a cherry.

## VODKATINI

2 parts vodka                                  I part dry vermouth

- Mix ingredients together and add a twist of lemon peel.
- A variation of the dry martini, vodka replacing gin.

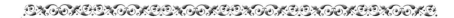

## VOLCANO

2/3 jigger vodka                               I jigger Southern Comfort
I/3 jigger light rum

- Shake with cracked ice.

## WHITE ELEPHANT

I oz. vodka                                    I oz. milk
I oz. Creme de Cacao

- Pour into a short glass with ice and stir.

## YELLOW FEVER

I½ oz. vodka                                   4 oz. lemonade

- Add vodka to a tall glass with ice. Fill with lemonade and stir.

# Some Favourite Sandals Drinks

## BLUE MONDAY

I measure vodka
I measure Blue Curacao
7 Up to strength

Dash of lime juice
Dash of Augustan Bitters

Method: Shake

## BLUE MURDER

I oz. tequila
I oz. Gold Rum
I oz. gin
Dash of lime juice

I oz. vodka
I oz. Blue Curacao
I oz. 7 Up

Method: Shake

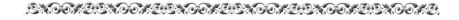

## COOL & NICE

I measure coconut rum
I measure apricot brandy
I oz. orange juice

I oz. pineapple juice
Clear syrup to taste

Method: Shake

# LOVE POTION

I measure Gold Rum
I measure Triple Sec
I oz. pineapple juice

I oz. orange juice
Strawberry syrup to taste
Dash of lime juice

Method: Shake

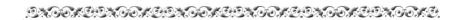

# SANDALS ICED TEA

I oz. rum
I oz. tequila
I oz. gin

I oz. vodka
I oz. Triple Sec
7 Up to taste

Method: Blend

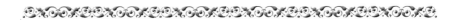

# SANDALS PINA COLADA

I measure Gold Rum
I measure coconut rum
Coconut cream

Milk
Pineapple juice

Method: Shake

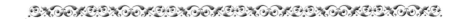

# VIRGINS KISS

I oz. Gold Rum
I oz. Blue Curacao
Orange juice

Pineapple juice
Clear syrup
Dash of Anisette

Method: Shake

**Note:** *On holidays at Sandals measurements per cocktails are at the bartenders' discretion. Happy mixing!*

# *Liqueur Based Drinks*

If one could only teach the English how to talk and the Irish how to listen, life might be civilized...

— *Oscar Wilde*

SANGSTER'S

JAMAICA RUM CREAM

ORIGINAL

Liqueur

# *Liqueurs*

# SANGSTER'S WORLD'S END

## BLUE MOON

1/6 part Old Jamaican Gold Rum           3/6 part milk
2/6 part Blue Mountain Coffee Liqueur

- Pour cracked ice into a blender and pour in the ingredients.
- Add one medium-sized ripe banana to each pint of milk used.
- Blend for two to three minutes until ingredients are smooth and foaming, then pour into cocktail glass.
- Add a dash of Sangster's Bitters.
- Sprinkle lightly with nutmeg or grated coconut and serve.

## BLUE RUSSIAN

½ part Blue Mountain Coffee Liqueur        ½ part vodka

- Put ice into a chilled old-fashioned glass.
- Pour first the vodka and then the Blue Mountain Coffee Liqueur over the ice.
- Stir and serve.

# CAFÉ KINGSTON

I part Sangster's Jamaica Rum Cream

Cream

4 parts hot coffee

Nutmeg

- Combine Sangster's Jamaica Rum Cream with hot coffee in a coffee cup.
- Float cream on top and sprinkle lightly with nutmeg.

# CIRRHOSIS-ON-THE-SEA

I measure Sangster's Coffee Liqueur

I measure Grand Marnier

I measure Appleton Dark Rum

¾ pt. fresh orange juice

Dash of lime juice

- Mix well together in a jug and serve in tall glasses with plenty ice.

# COFFEE A LA BLUE MOUNTAIN

I oz. brandy

½ oz. 151-proof rum

I oz. Sangster's Coffee Liqueur

½ oz. Curacao

Hot coffee

Whipped cream

- Pour the brandy, rum, coffee liqueur and Curacao into a 14 oz. hurricane glass, having first dipped the rum into sugar, if you wish.
- Fill to within an inch of the top with the rich, full-bodied coffee, and top with a blob of whipped cream.

CAFÉ KINGSTON (page 58)

# COFFEE A LA MIKE

1½ oz. Sangster's Coffee Liqueur
¼ oz. white Créme de Menthe

Hot coffee
Whipped cream

- Pour the Sangster's Coffee Liqueur and créme de Menthe into an 8 or 10 oz. pedestal mug.
- Fill to within an inch of the rim with a rich, full-bodied Jamaican Blue Mountain Coffee.
- Top with a blob of whipped cream.

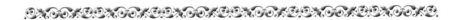

# COFFEE COCONUT

1 oz. Sangster's Blue Mountain Coffee Liqueur
Nutmeg
1 coconut

3 cubes ice
2 oz. brandy

- Take top off coconut and remove milk.
- Place half the milk and ice cubes into cocktail shaker, then add brandy and Coffee Liqueur.
- Shake and strain back into the coconut.
- Dust with nutmeg and serve with spoon and drinking straws.

# COFFEE EGG NOG
An old-fashioned favourite with a delightful difference.

2 parts Sangster's Coffee Liqueur
1 part brandy
2 parts milk

1 egg (beaten)
1 teaspoon sugar

- Beat egg, blend in Sangster's Coffee Liqueur, milk and sugar, and pour over cracked ice.
- Sprinkle with nutmeg. As a nightcap, serve warm.

# COFFEE 'N COLA

- Pour 1½ ozs. Sangster's Coffee Liqueur over ice in a tall glass. Fill with cola and serve.

## COFFEE ON-THE-ROCKS

- Pour a generous measure of Sangster's Coffee Liqueur over ice.
- For a little zip, add a touch of vodka.

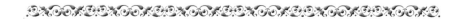

## COOL MULE

¼ part Sangster's Blue Mountain Coffee Liqueur        ¼ part Old Jamaica Gold Rum
½ part Vanilla ice cream

- Blend the ingredients until smooth and frothy.
- Pour into a tall glass and serve with a cherry.

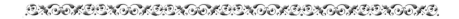

## JAMAICAN COFFEE

1 oz. Sangster's Coffee Liqueur        Hot Coffee
¾ oz. Appleton Rum

- Serve in mug, slightly sweetened.
- Top with whipped cream and sprinkle with nutmeg.

## JAMAICA HOP

1/3 part Blue Mountain Coffee Liqueur        1/3 part light cream
1/3 part white Créme de Cacao

- Shake well with ice. Serve in a stemmed glass.
- A smooth taste to delight you — on the beach or at the bar.

MONKEY'S UNCLE (page 63)

## MADGE

1 oz. brandy
1 oz. Sangster's Coffee Liqueur
1 oz. Créme de Cacao

Hot coffee
Whipped cream

- Pour the brandy, coffee liqueur and créme de cacao into an 8 or 10 oz. pedestal mug.
- Fill to within an inch of the rim with a rich, full- bodied Jamaican coffee.
- Top with a blob of whipped cream.

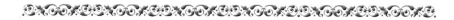

## MEXICAN COFFEE

1 oz. tequila
1 oz. Sangster's Coffee Liqueur
Powdered cinnamon (optional garnish)

Whipped cream
Hot coffee

- Pour the tequila and coffee liqueur into an 8 or 10 oz. pedestal mug.
- Fill to within an inch of the rim with a rich, full-bodied coffee.
- Top with whipped cream, sprinkled with cinnamon if you wish.

## MONKEY'S UNCLE

2 parts Sangster's Jamaica Rum Cream
1 part Appleton Estate VX Jamaica Rum

1 part Crème de Banana

- Combine ingredients with cubed ice, shake and strain into martini glass.

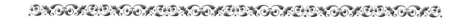

## NUTTY PROFESSOR

3 parts Sangster's Jamaica Rum Cream

1 part Frangelico hazelnut liqueur

- Combine all ingredients in a rock glass over ice.

**NUTTY PROFESSOR** (page 63)

## SANGSTER'S DELIGHT

I oz. Blue Mountain Coffee Liqueur
I ripe banana

I dash lime juice
I bar spoon simple syrup

- Blend with crushed ice. Serve in a brandy snifter with a short straw.
- An exclusive Caribbean drink that's naturally good tasting.

## TANGERINE DREAM

2 parts Sangster's Jamaica Rum Cream

I part Grand Marnier

- Chill ingredients and layer in a shooter glass.

## TROPICAL COFFEE

I part Sangster's Coffee Liqueur
I part lime juice

4 parts tonic water

- Pour ingredients into a highball glass filled with ice and a slice of lime.

SANGSTER'S ICE-CREAM (page )

# Rum Liqueur

## BLACK PEARL

I measure Rum Liqueur
I measure cognac

Champagne

- Chill a champagne glass.
- Pour in the Rum Liqueur and cognac and top up to brim with champagne.
- Add cracked ice and garnish with a black cherry.

## BLUE MOUNTAIN COW

I measure Rum Liqueur
I egg

2 cups ice cold milk

- Whisk the egg into the cold milk until it is thoroughly mixed.
- Pour the creamy mixture into a tall glass with Rum Liqueur.
- Stir gently and serve.

## CAFE CALYPSO (HOT)

4 cups freshly percolated coffee
8 tablespoons dark rum

12 tablespoons Rum Liqueur
¼ pt. whipped cream

- Blend the Rum Liqueur and rum gently with the coffee in a heat-proof jug. The coffee should be hot but not boiling.
- Serve the drink in large coffee cups, sweetening slightly with castor sugar and top with whipped cream.

# DIANA'S DELIGHT

Coffee ice cream
Vanilla ice cream
Black coffee

Rum Liqueur
Egg whites
Toasted chopped almonds

- Pour into a tall parfait glass a layer of chilled black coffee laced with Rum Liqueur.
- Add successive layers of vanilla ice-cream, whipped egg white sweetened with sugar and finally a scoop of coffee ice-cream.
- Garnish with chopped almonds and pour Rum Liqueur on top.

# IRISH COFFEE

2 tablespoons Rum Liqueur
2 teaspoons fine granulated sugar

Black coffee
Whipped cream

- Rinse a large wine glass with warm water, and add sugar and fill glass about 2/3 full with hot, strong, black coffee.
- Stir. Then add Rum Liqueur and top with a spoonful of softly whipped cream.

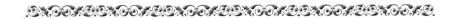

# JAMAICA COW

I part Rum Liqueur

4 parts milk

- Pour one measure of Rum Liqueur into a highball glass and top up with ice cold milk.
- Add ice cubes and stir gently.

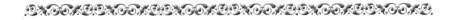

# JAMAICA SKIP

I oz. Rum Liqueur
I oz. Créme de Cacao

I oz. light cream

- Shake well with ice and strain into a cocktail glass.

## MORNING MIST

- Rum Liqueur on the rocks…
- With a squeeze of lime…
- Delightfully different.

## ORANGE DAWN

I part Rum Liqueur                    4 parts fresh orange juice

- Serve with plenty ice.

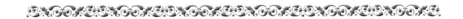

## PARFAIT A RHUM

¼ cup Rum Liqueur                    ¼ cup sugar
¼ cup strong, clear coffee           I egg
¼ cup evaporated milk, chilled       Pinch salt
½ teaspoon vanilla

- Cook sugar and coffee together at 230° F, or until syrup spins a thread.
- Add salt to egg and beat until stiff but not dry.
- Add Rum Liqueur to syrup.
- Pour syrup slowly into egg white, beating constantly.
- Chill and whip milk until very stiff.
- Fold in egg white and vanilla. Freeze until firm. (Serves 6)

# Coffee Liqueurs

## BLACK RUSSIAN

The internationally acclaimed drink of connoisseurs.

I part Blue Mountain Coffee Liqueur
I part vodka
2 or 3 ice cubes

- Stir well, then sip and enjoy.

## BROWN COW

Pour I oz. Coffee Liqueur over ice

- Fill with fresh milk and serve. As a special treat, add nutmeg.

## KAHLUA 'N SODA

- Pour I½ oz. Kahlua over ice in a highball glass and add three drops of lemon juice.
- Fill with club soda; decorate with lemon slice. For a little zip, add a touch of vodka.

## KAHLUA ORANGE

- Pour I oz. Kahlua over ice and top up with fresh orange juice.
- Decorate with orange slice, if desired.

# TIA ALEXANDRA

I part Tia Maria
I part cognac
I part fresh cream

- Shake with cracked ice, strain and serve. For elegant entertaining, offer your friends a Tia Alexandra, a remarkably smooth and delicious-tasting drink.

# T'N'T

*A new discovery in delicious refreshment.*

- Pour 1½ oz. Tia Maria over ice in a tall glass.
- Top up with tonic. Decorate with lemon slice if desired.

# V/X JAMAICAN COFFEE

I ½ oz. Appleton Estate V/X Jamaican Rum
Hot black coffee
Splash of whipped cream

- Combine V/X and coffee in coffee mug.
- Top with whipped cream.

**V/X JAMAICAN COFFEE** (page 71)

# *Pimento Liqueur*

## ANTIGUA STINGER

1 ½ oz. pimento liqueur         1½ oz. grapefruit juice
2 oz. club soda

* Serve in a highball glass with ice.

## BARBADOS SOUR

¾ oz. pimento liqueur         1½ oz. cognac

* Shake well with cracked ice.

## PIMENTO SOUR

1½ oz. pimento liqueur         ¾ oz. fresh lemon juice
2 oz. club soda

* Serve in a highball glass with ice.

## ROSE HALL LIQUEUR

1½ oz. pimento liqueur         2 oz. club soda
1½ oz. orange juice

* Serve in a highball glass with ice.

## ST. LUCIA JUMP-UP

1½ oz. pimento liqueur                               2 oz. club soda
1½ oz. pineapple juice

- Serve in a highball glass with ice.

## WHITE SWAN

1¾ oz pimento liqueur                               3 oz. milk

- Put in blender with crushed ice for a few seconds and serve in a champagne glass.

# Whisky Based Drinks

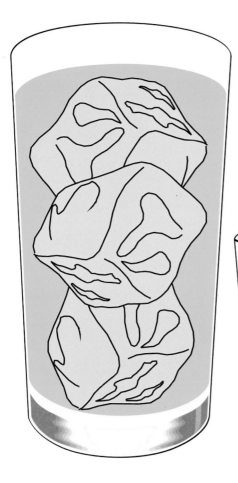

McPherson, being drunk, fell down a dark staircase. He had a half bottle of whisky in his hip pocket and unfortunately it broke. Finding liquid on his hands, he muttered: "I hope tae God it's blood.'

# ARTIST'S SPECIAL

1/3 part Whisky
1/3 part sherry

1/6 part lemon juice
1/6 part sugar syrup

- Stir well with ice and strain into glass.

# BLINKER COCKTAIL

½ oz. Canadian Whisky
1/4 oz. grenadine

¼ oz. grapefruit juice
Cracked ice

- Shake whisky, grapefruit juice and grenadine with cracked ice.
- Serve in chilled cocktail glass.

# BOBBY BURNS

½ part Scotch whisky
¼ part dry vermouth
¼ part sweet vermouth

I dash Benedictine
Ice cubes
Lemon peel

- Stir Scotch, dry and sweet vermouth and Benedictine with ice.
- Serve in 2½ oz. cocktail glass.
- Garnish with twist of lemon peel.

# CREOLE

½ part Whisky
½ partsweet vermouth

2 dash Benedictine
2 dash Amer Picon

- Stir with ice and strain into glass.
- Serve with twist of lemon peel.

## DUPPY

- Pour 6 jiggers of whisky into a mixing glass and add a few cloves. Let soak about 1 hour.
- Add 5 or 6 drops orange bitters and 1 jigger Curacao.
- Shake well with ice and strain into glasses. Serves 6.

## FLU

2 jiggers Rye Whisky
1 teaspoon ginger brandy
1 teaspoon Rock Candy syrup

1 dollop Jamaica Rum
Juice of ¼ lemon

- Stir well without ice and strain into glass.

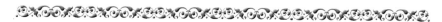

## HOT DECK

¾ part Rye Whisky
¼ part sweet vermouth

1 dash Jamaican ginger

- Shake well with ice and strain into glass.

## HOT FLASHES

2 oz. Whisky
½ oz. Campari
Lemon peel

¼ oz. Bianco Vermouth
Ice

- Mix whisky, Campari and vermouth with ice in a mixing glass.
- Serve with lemon peel in a cocktail glass.

## LINSTEAD

1 part Scotch whisky

1 part sweetened pineapple juice

- Shake together with a dash of Pastis and add a twist of lemon peel.

# MAMIE TAYLOR

2 oz. Scotch whisky
Ice

Ginger ale
Slice of lemon

- Serve scotch in 10 oz. glass with ice. Top with ginger ale and slice of lemon.

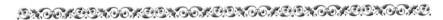

# MANHATTAN (DRY)

1½ oz. Canadian Whisky
¾ oz. dry vermouth
1 or 2 dash Angostura Bitters (optional)

Ice
Twist of lemon or olive

- Stir whisky, vermouth and bitters with ice and strain into 3 oz. cocktail glass.
- Add twist of lemon peel or olive and serve.

# MANHATTAN (MEDIUM)

4 parts Rye (Canadian) Whisky
1 part dry vermouth

1 part sweet vermouth

- Mix together and serve.

# MANHATTAN (SWEET)

1½ oz. Canadian Whisky
¾ oz. sweet vermouth
1 dash Angostura Bitters (optional).

Ice
Maraschino cherry

- Stir whisky, vermouth and bitters with ice and strain into 3 oz. cocktail glass.
- Garnish with maraschino cherry.

# MODERN NO. 2

2 jiggers Scotch whisky
1 dash lemon juice
1 dash Pernod

2 dash Jamaican Rum
1 dash orange bitters

- Stir well with ice, strain into glass and serve with a cherry.

# MORNING GLORY

1½ oz. Scotch whisky
White of egg
Soda water

1 teaspoon castor sugar
Ice

- Shake Scotch, egg white and castor sugar, then strain into a highball glass with ice.
- Top with soda water and serve.

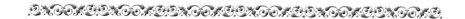

# OLD-FASHIONED

- Pour into a tumbler 1 – 2 teaspoonfuls sugar syrup and add 1–3 dash of Angostura.
- Stir to blend them. Add a little rye or Bourbon and stir again.
- Add 2 large ice cubes. Stir.
- Fill with more whisky nearly to the top. Stir. Add a zest of lemon to the glass.
- Decorate with a cherry and serve with a spoon to stir further.

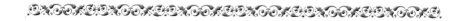

# ROB ROY

½ part Scotch Whisky
½ part sweet vermouth

1 dash Angostura Bitters
1 maraschino cherry

- Stir scotch, vermouth and bitters in mixing glass with ice.
- Pour into 2 oz. cocktail glass, add cherry and serve.

# RUSTY NAIL

- Pour 2 parts Scotch whisky and I part Drambuie over ice in old fashioned glass.
- Serve with a twist of lemon peel.

# WHISKY COCKTAIL

4 parts Scotch whisky
I part Orange Curacao

2 dash Angostura Bitters

- Mix together, add a cherry and serve.

# WHISKY MILK PUNCH

2 oz. Scotch whisky
½ pint milk

1½ teaspoons sugar
Nutmeg

- Shake Scotch, milk and sugar with ice and strain into a highball glass.
- Sprinkle nutmeg on top and serve.

# WHISKY-ON-THE-ROCKS

- Serve 2 oz. Scotch whisky in old fashioned glass with ice cubes.

# WHIZZ BANG

2 parts Scotch whisky
I part dry vermouth
2 dash Orange Bitters

2 dash Pastis
2 dash grenadine

- Mix together and serve.

## THE DONKEY

A man walks into a large bar on the hip strip in Montego Bay. He sits down and orders a drink.

He then notices a jar that is full of money. The man asks the bartender what the jar is for. The bartender then says that he has a donkey in the back room and if anyone can make him laugh they win the money. If not they owe him $100 dollars.

The man responds, "I can do it!"

So he goes into the back room and about 5 minutes later, the bartender hears the donkey laughing out loud. The man walks out and takes the money from the jar, thanks the bartender, and leaves.

About a month later, the man comes back into the bar and there is a new jar of money. The man asks the bartender what the new jar of money is for.

The bartender looks at the man and says, "If you can make the donkey cry, the money is yours, if not you owe me $100 dollars."

The man says, "Ok, I'll do it!

He walks into the back room and about 2 minutes goes by when the bartender hears the donkey crying. The man walks out and grabs the money out of the jar, but before the man leaves, the bartender asks, "How did you make the donkey laugh?"

The man looks at the bartender and says, "Well, the first time I told the donkey that I had a bigger pecker then he did."

"How did you make him cry?" ask the bartender?

"Well, I showed him."

# Brandy Based Drinks

Not an ascent from body to spirit, but the descent of spirit into body.

– N. O. Brown.

## BETWEEN-THE-SHEETS

1/3 part brandy
1/3 part light rum

1/3 part Cointreau

• Shake well with ice and strain into glass.

## BOSOM CARESSER

2/3 part brandy
1/3 part orange Curacao

Yolk of I egg
I teaspoon grenadine

• Shake together brandy, Curacao, egg yolk and grenadine.
• Pour into 3 oz. cocktail glass and serve.

## BRANDY ALEXANDER

1/3 part brandy
1/3 part fresh cream

1/3 part Créme de Cacao
Nutmeg

• Shake brandy, Créme de Cacao and fresh cream with ice.
• Strain into 6 oz. champagne glass.  Serve with nutmeg sprinkled on top.

## CARNIVAL

I part brandy
I part apricot brandy
I dash orange juice

I part Lillet
I dash Kirsch

• Shake together and serve.

## CHERRY BLOSSOM

2 parts brandy
3 parts cherry brandy
I dash grenadine

I dash orange Curacao
I dash lemon juice

• Shake together and serve.

## CITY SLICKER

2/3 part brandy                                    I dash Pernod
1/3 part Curacao

- Shake well with ice and strain into glass.

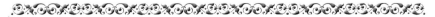

## COFFEE COCKTAIL

1 1/3 oz. brandy                          1 1/3 oz. green Créme de Menthe

- Shake brandy and Créme de Menthe.
- Strain into 3 oz. cocktail glass and serve.

## COFFEE COCONUT

1 oz. brandy                              1 oz. Sangster's Coffee Liqueur
1 coconut                                 3 cubes ice
Nutmeg

- Take off top of coconut and remove milk.
- Place half the milk and ice cubes into cocktail shaker.
- Add brandy and Tia Maria, then shake and strain back into the coconut.
- Dust with nutmeg and serve with spoon and drinking straws.

## DEVIL COCKTAIL

1 1/3 oz. brandy                          1 1/3 Créme de Menthe

- Shake brandy and Créme de Menthe and strain into 3 oz. cocktail glass and serve.

# FRENCH CONNECTION

1½ oz. dry gin
I teaspoon powdered sugar
Juice of ½ lemon

3 oz. champagne
Cracked ice
Twist of lemon

- Combine gin, sugar, lemon juice and shake with ice.
- Strain into 12" highball glass containing ice.
- Fill with champagne and add twist of lemon to serve.

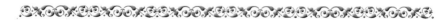

# GRENADIER

2/3 brandy
1/3 ginger brandy

I dash Jamaican ginger
I teaspoon powdered sugar

- Stir well with ice and strain into glass.

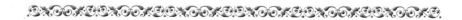

# HORSE'S NECK

1½ oz. brandy
2 dash Angostura Bitters
4 cubes ice

I lemon
Dry ginger ale

- Peel the skin of lemon in one piece. Place one end of the peel over the edge of a 10 oz. highball glass (giving the effect of a horse's neck).
- Fill glass with ice cubes. Add brandy and Angostura Bitters, top dry ginger ale and serve.

# JAMAICA GRANITO

1½ oz. Jamaican Brandy
I small scoop lemon or orange sherbet

I oz. Curacao

- Combine in collins glass and fill balance with carbonated water and stir.
- Sprinkle nutmeg on top.

## BODY PARTS

*There was a lady at a bar in Kingston. Every time she wanted a drink, she would raise her hand. She had very bad armpit hair. The Bartender was getting really grossed out and told the man sitting at the bar that next time she did that, he was not going to give her a drink.*

*One minute later she said, "Bartender, bartender, get me another drink."*

*The bartender told her no. The man sitting there said, "Oh give the poor ballerina another drink."*

*The bartender said, "How do you know she is a ballerina?"*

*The man replied, "Well anyone that can lift their leg that high must be a ballerina!"*

## DESIGNATED DECOY

*One night, a Jamaican police officer was stalking out a particularly rowdy bar in Kingston for possible violations of the driving under the influence laws.*

*At closing time, he saw a young man stumble out of the bar, trip on the curb, and try his keys on five different cars before he found his. Then, the man sat in the front seat fumbling around with his keys for several minutes. Everyone left the bar and drove off. Finally, he started his engine and began to pull away.*

*The police officer was waiting for him. He stopped the driver, read him his rights and administered the Breathalyzer test. The results showed a reading of 0.0. The puzzled officer demanded to know how that could be.*

*The driver replied, "Tonight, I'm the Designated Decoy."*

# Campari Based Drinks

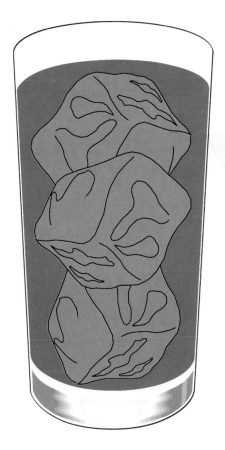

*As if you could kill time without injuring eternity.*

*Thoreau.*

# AMERICANO

- Pour I oz. Campari and I oz. Italian vermouth over cracked ice.
- Add a twist of lemon peel.

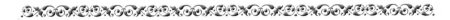

# CAMPARI & SODA

- Pour 2 oz. Campari over ice in a tall glass.
- Fill with soda and stir.

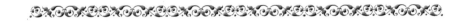

# CAMPARI & TONIC

- Pour 2 oz. Campari over ice in a tall glass.
- Fill with tonic water and serve.

# FRONT END LIFTER

- Pour I ½ oz. White Overproof Rum and top up with Campari.

# LENA COCKTAIL
(Winner of the International Cocktail Competition held in Tokyo in 1971.)

| | |
|---|---|
| 5/10 part Bourbon | 1/10 part Campari |
| 2/10 part Martini Rossi vermouth | 1/10 part Galliano |
| 1/10 part dry vermouth | I maraschino cherry |

- Stir bourbon, M.R. vermouth and dry vermouth, Campari and Galliano in mixing glass.
- Serve with cherry.

## MIKE'S DELIGHT

- Mix equal parts of Campari and grapefruit juice and serve with ice.
- Top off with a cherry.

## NEGRONI

1 oz. Campari                                      1 oz. Italian sweet vermouth
1 oz. gin

- Shake ingredients with ice and strain into a cocktail glass.
- Stir and serve.

# Beer Based Drinks

The local publican once acted as an usher at a funeral and asked the mourners to pass around the bier.

# Beers Of Jamaica

## Kingston Beer...

Jamaica no longer has to look to foreign shores to satisfy its discerning palate. Brewed in the fine tradition of a classic Pilsner Beer , KINGSTON is a beer with a golden hue, distinct aroma, and a full strong hop flavour. This premium beer born right here on the "Rock" has been crafted under the expert guidance of our Brew Masters, Tony Kelly and Neil Glasgow, to be a culmination of everything Jamaican. Our Jamaican heritage including our independence, the colours of our flag, and our symbol of strength (the crocodile) all together with the 'rude' swagger of our people (our consumers) make Kingston Pilsner Beer (named after our capital) the ultimate Jamaican beverage which offers all these elements in a crisp, clean refreshing drink that is best when served ice COLD!!

## Red Stripe Beer...

The Jamaican beer of world renown first brewed in 1928, Red Stripe Beer is made from malt corn hops and water. Like many cities who have built their reputation on beer, i.e. Copenhagen in Denmark, Amsterdam in Holland, Burton-on-Trent in England, Munich in West Germany, Milwaukee in the U. S. A., Kingston has built its name on Red Stripe; a beer of international reputation.

# BEER BUSTER

Ice cold beer
1½ oz. 100 proof vodka

2 dash Tabasco Sauce

- Put vodka in a highball glass and fill up with beer.
- Add Tabasco Sauce and stir lightly,

# BEER CUP

1 bottle lager beer
1½ oz. gin
Juice of ½ lemon

1 bottle ginger beer
Soda water
Slice of cucumber

- Mix together beer, gin, ginger beer and lemon juice and a splash of soda water.
- Garnish with a cucumber slice and a sprig of mint.
- Add ice and stir slightly.

# BLUE MOUNTAIN PUNCH

3 pts. warmed beer
1 teaspoon Jamaican powdered ginger
1 teaspoon grated nutmeg

¼ pt. rum
3 eggs
2 tablespoons molasses

- Blend ginger and nutmeg with 2½ pts. beer and beat.
- Beat eggs with remaining ½ pt. beer and molasses.
- Mix the two together, a little at a time, continuously beating and adding the rum at the same time.

# BOILERMAKER

- 1 large jigger of Scotch whisky served straight with a glass of beer as a chaser.

# CARROT PUNCH

1 pt. beer
1½ pts. water

6 medium carrots (grated)
1 cup condensed milk

- Make carrot juice, using water.
- Sweeten with condensed milk.
- Add beer and a dash of bitters. Serve chilled over ice cubes.

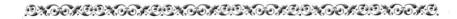

# CHOCOLATE BEER MALT

3 pts.beer
6 scoops ice cream (chocolate)

1 tin condensed milk

- Mix the beer and milk together. Pour in blender and mix at medium speed.
- Add ice cream and crushed ice.
- Mix at high speed until mixture thickens.  Serve immediately.

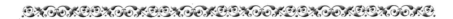

# KOLA BEER

1 pt. lager beer
½ pt. Cola

6 ice cubes

- Pour beer in a beer mug and top up with cola.
- Add ice cubes and stir lightly.

# POLICEMAN GLOW

1 pt. Red Stripe beer
3 jiggers rum

1 tin pineapple juice
Pinch of nutmeg or cinnamon

- Mix all ingredients, shake well.
- Pour crushed ice in old-fashioned glasses.
- Garnish with orange or pineapple slice.

# RED EYE

½ cold beer                    ½ tomato juice

* Mix beer with tomato juice and serve in 10 oz. glass.
* A good pick drink for those 'mornings after.'

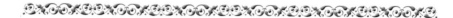

# RED STRIPE COOLER

8 oz. Red Stripe beer          ½ teaspoon lime juice
8 oz. tomato juice

* Mix ingredients together. Serve on ice in a tall glass.

# SHANDY

½ beer                         ½ lemonade

* Mix beer with ice cold lemonade.

# WOODPECKER

¾ cup beer                     3 tablespoons sugar
2 medium mangoes               1 tablespoon lime juice
3 slices pineapple             3 cups water
1¼ cups orange juice

* Blend together mango, pineapple slices, orange juice and sugar.
* Pour into large jug, add water and beer.
* Serve in long, slender glasses over crushed ice with a twist of lime peel.

# Other Assorted Drinks

'Sarah,' said Abe, 'call a vet. I am sick.' 'I'll call a doctor,' 'I don't want de doctor I want a vet.' 'Vy a vet?' 'I vork like a horse, live like a dog, and sleep with a cow.'

# ALCAPULCO

1 jigger Tequila
1 jigger Jamaica rum

2 jiggers pineapple juice
½ jigger grapefruit juice

- Shake well with ice cubes.

# ARTILLERY PUNCH

1 quart strong black tea
1 quart rye whisky
1 bottle red wine
1 pint Jamaica rum
½ pint dry gin

½ pint brandy
1 jigger Benedictine
1 pint orange juice
½ pint lemon juice

- Combine all ingredients in a large punch bowl with a block of ice.
- Add sugar syrup if punch is too dry. Decorate with twists of lemon peel. Makes 25 to 30 cups.

# BAMBOO

½ sherry
1 dash Angostura Bitters

½ sweet vermouth

- Stir well with ice and strain into glass,

# BISHOP'S COOLER

2 jiggers Burgundy
1 teaspoon sugar
2 dash Angostura Bitters

1/3 jigger lemon juice
½ jigger Appleton Dark Rum
1/3 jigger orange juice

- Place in large highball glass, fill with shaved ice, stir well and serve.

# BLACK POWER

2 oz. Marsala (dessert wine)          3 cubes ice
Coca – Cola                           Slice of lemon

- Top Marsala with Coca-Cola over ice cubes in old-fashioned glass.
- Add slice of lemon and serve.

# BLOODY BULL

I jigger Tequila                      ½ jigger lemon juice
Dash of Worcestershire and Tabasco

- Mix over ice in large glass.
- Fill with Bouillon and tomato juice, half and half.

# CHARLES COCKTAIL

1½ oz. sweet vermouth                 I dash bitters
1½ oz. brandy

- Shake with ice and strain into old-fashioned glass over ice cubes.

# FESTIVAL PUNCH

2 teaspoons ground all spice(pimento)    I quart Jamaica rum
I quart sweet apple cider                I or 2 tablespoons butter
2 or 3 sticks cinnamon, broken

- Heat ingredients in a heavy saucepan until almost boiling.
- Serve hot in mugs. Serves about 10.

## FISH HOUSE PUNCH

A celebrated Philadelphia Club recipe of 1732.

12 oz. sugar

3 pints water

1½ pints lemon juice

2 bottles rum

1 bottle grape brandy

4½ oz. peach brandy

- Dissolve the sugar in a little water in the punchbowl.
- Add the lemon and the rest of the water, stirring well.
- Add the rum, grape brandy and peach brandy.
- Stir and allow to stand for several hours.
- Before serving put a big block of ice in the bowl. Serve when cold.

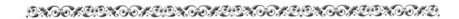

## GLOGG

Pour the following into a kettle:

2 bottles wine (port, sherry, claret, burgundy or Madeira).

2 oz. dried orange peel

Insert cheese cloth bag containing:

25 cloves

20 cardamom seeds

2 oz. dried orange peel

2 oz. cinnamon sticks

- Boil slowly for 15 minutes, stirring occasionally.
- Add one pound each blanched almonds and seedless raisins and continue to boil for additional 15 minutes.
- Remove kettle from stove and place wire grill containing one pound lump sugar over opening. Pour 1/5 of brandy over sugar making sure to saturate all of it.
- Light sugar with match and let it flame.
- After sugar has melted, replace kettle cover to extinguish flame.
- Stir again and remove spice bag. Serve hot in punch cups with a few almonds and raisins.

## GROG

- A toddy made with dark rum and lemon juice.
- A hot-buttered rum is similar, with a slice of butter instead of lemon juice.

# GRASSHOPPER

⅔ jigger green Créme de Menthe
⅔ jigger white Créme de Cacao

2/3 jigger cream

- Shake well with ice and serve in champagne glass.

# GRIM CHASER

¼ part Grand Marnier
¼ part Curacao

¼ part lemon juice
¼ part grenadine

- Stir well with ice and Strain into glass.

# HOT BUTTERED RUM

2 jiggers Jamaica Rum
I twist lemon peel
2 sticks cinnamon

I or 2 cloves
Boiling cider
Butter

- Place rum, lemon peel, clove and cinnamon in a pewter tankard or heavy mug.
- Fill with boiling cider. Float a pat of butter on top and stir well.

# HOT PANTS

I½ oz. Tequila
2 oz. peppermint schnapps
I teaspoon powdered sugar

I tablespoon unsweetened
grapefruit juice

- Shake with ice cubes and pour into old-fashioned glass rimmed with salt.

# HUMPTY DUMPTY

2/3 part dry vermouth

1/3 part Maraschino

- Stir well with ice and strain into glass.

# LIMEY

1 oz. Appleton Rum
1 oz. lime liqueur

½ oz. Curacao
2 teaspoons lime juice

- Combine ingredients with half a cup of crushed ice in a blender.
- Blend at low speed and pour into champagne glass.
- Add a twist of lime peel.

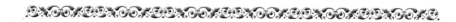

# LOLLYPOP GIRL

2 jiggers Cointreau
2 jiggers Chartreuse

2 jiggers Kirsch
1 dash Maraschino

- Shake well with ice and strain into glasses. Serve after dinner.

# PANTOMIME

1 jigger dry vermouth
1 egg white

1 dash grenadine
1 dash Orgeat syrup

- Shake well with ice and strain into glass.

## PERFECT

I jigger dry vermouth                                    I jigger dry gin
I jigger sweet vermouth

- Stir well with ice and strain into glass.
- Serve with twist of lemon peel.

## PICADOR

2 parts Tequila
I part Kahlua or Tia Maria or Sangster's Blue Mountain Coffee Liqueur.

- Stir well and add ice.

## SANTA CRUZ RUM DAISY

- Fill a goblet 1/3 full of shaved ice and add 3 dash of sugar syrup, 3 dash Maraschino or Curacao, juice of ½ lemon and fill with rum.
- Shake well and strain into glass.

## SONS OF NEGUS

- Heat I bottle of Sherry or Port and place in a pitcher.
- Rub a little lemon rind on 6 cubes of sugar and add to the mixture.
- Also add 2 - 3 large twists of rind and the juice of I lemon.
- Add 10 drops of vanilla and 2 cups of boiling water.
- Sweeten to taste if necessary and strain into glasses.
- Add a grating of nutmeg and serve. Makes 8 cups.

## SORREL APPETIZER

1 lb. prepared sorrel                          6 pts. boiling water
2 oz. grated green ginger

- Mix ingredients together, cover and leave overnight.
- Strain and add rum and sugar to taste.
- Serve over crushed ice.

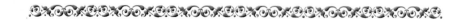

## SPANISH TOWN COCKTAIL

2 oz. Appleton Rum                          1 teaspoon Triple Sec

- Stir with ice and strain into cocktail glass.

## SPECIAL JAMAICAN RUM PUNCH (HOT)

1 bottle rum                          1 bottle brandy
2 lemons                               ½ bottle sherry
4 oz. sugar                            1 teaspoonful ginger
Up to 3½ pints boiling water          Grated nutmeg

- Grate the rind of the lemons into a small earthenware bowl and add sugar.
- Macerate sugar and lemon gratings, add the juice of lemons and the ginger.
- Mix well and place in another large earthenware bowl previously heated.
- Then add, in the following order: rum, brandy, sherry and boiling water.
- Mix well, sweeten further if desired and stand near heat for 20 minutes before serving in glasses of mugs, with a grating of nutmeg on top.

## WEST INDIAN PUNCH

2 qts. rum
1/5 Créme de Banana
1 qt. pineapple juice
1 qt. orange juice
1 qt. lemon juice

¾ cup powdered sugar
1 teaspoon grated nutmeg
1 teaspoon cinnamon
½ teaspoon grated cloves

- Dissolve sugar and spices in 6 oz. carbonated water.
- Pour into large punch-bowl over block of ice, and add other ingredients.
- Stir and decorate with sliced bananas.

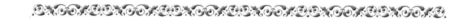

## ZOMBIE

2 oz. light rum
1 oz. Jamaican rum
½ oz. apricot brandy
½ teaspoon powdered sugar
½ oz. lemon juice
½ oz. 150° proof Demerara Rum
Mint, pineapple, cherry for decoration
Shaved ice and cracked ice
1 tablespoon (or 1 teaspoon) Papaya nectar and/or
1 bar-spoon pineapple juice and/or
1 bar-spoon passion fruit juice and/or
1 bar-spoon plum or apricot juice

- Fill 14 oz. zombie glass with shaved ice.
- In cocktail shaker put all above ingredients, except Demerara Rum and shake well with cracked ice.
- Pour unstrained into 14 oz. zombie glass which is ½ full of cracked ice.
- Decorate with sprig of mint or pineapple spear and cherry.
- Top with Demarara Rum, being careful to pour so that it floats on surface of drink.
- Serve with drinking straws.

# *Popular Jamaican Dancehall Mixes*

## Red Bull Energy Drink...

Originally from the country of Thailand but adapted by the Austrians, Red Bull has now become popular world wide and is one of the most frequently used base ingredients in drink mixes on the dancehall scene in Jamaica. Some of the most popular mixes include:

### DANCEHALL CRAZE

2 oz. Hennessy

I can Red Bull

- Pour Hennessy into cocktail glass and top up with Red Bull.

### GHETTO WHISKY

I can Red Bull

I bottle Stone Ginger Wine

- Pour Stone Ginger Wine in rock glass and top up with Red Bull.

## LIQUID VIAGRA (MIKE'S FAVOURITE)

I can Red Bull                                    I bottle Guinness

- Pour Guinness in rock glass and top up with Red Bull.

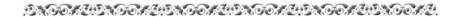

## REGGAE SUN RISER (DAWN'S OTHER SURPRISE)

2 oz. Champagne                                   I can Red Bull

- Pour champagne into cocktail glass and top up with Red Bull.

## TEAR UP DRAWS

I can Red Bull                                    I bottle Magnum

- Pour equal portions of each drink in a shaker and serve in a rock glass.
* Magnum - Tonic Wine.

* Top up with Red Bull according to taste.

# Non Alcoholic Drinks

He walked in Flavin's Bar and asked for a glass of water. He drank it and walked out. The next day he returned and did the same.

'Here' complained the barman, 'You come in here, ask for a glass of water, drink it and then walk…'

'What do you want me to do… stagger?'

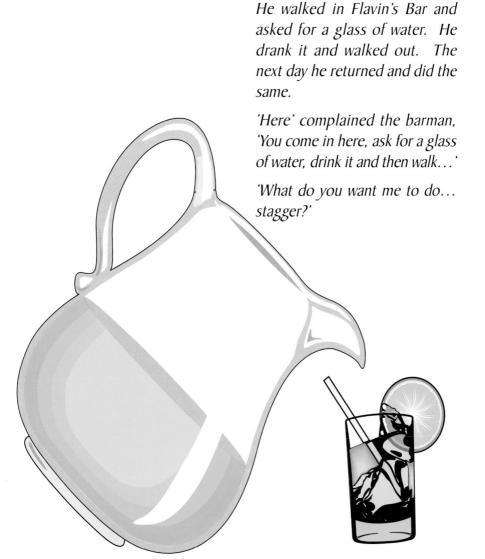

# BOO BOO'S SPECIAL

3 oz. pineapple juice
3 oz. orange juice
¼ lemon juice
Water

I dash Angostura Bitters
I dash grenadine
Pineapple or fruit in season
Ice

- In cocktail shaker with ice, mix lemon, pineapple and orange juices, Angostura bitters and grenadine.
- Shake and serve in tall highball glass. Garnish with pineapple or fruit in season.

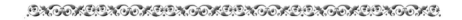

# HIMBERSHAFT

- I part raspberry syrup to 4 parts soda water.

# JUDY'S PUNCH (APPROX. 20 DRINKS)
Any fruit in season or 2 tins fruit salad in punch bowl.

Add cracked ice
8 dash Angostura Bitters
32 oz. soda water

I3 oz. lemon cordial
32 oz. lemonade
2 ozs. grenadine for Colour

- Mix ingredients and serve with fruit from bowl.

# LEMONADE

Juice of I lemon
2 tablespoons sugar
Cracked ice

I slice lemon
Water

- Fill tall glass with cracked ice and add lemon juice and sugar.
- Shake and pour unstrained into glass.
- Top with water. Slice lemon in drink. Serve with drinking straws

## LIMEADE

Juice of 3 limes
3 teaspoons powdered sugar
Water

1 maraschino cherry
Cracked ice

- Fill tall glass with cracked ice and add lime juice and sugar.
- Top with water and mix thoroughly.
- Garnish with cherry and serve with drinking straws.

## MICKEY MOUSE

Ice
Coca-Cola

Whipped cream
1 scoop ice cream

- Pour Coca-Cola in tall glass with ice.
- Add 1 scoop ice cream. Top with whipped cream.
- Serve with 2 cherries, drinking straw and spoon.

## NASEBERRY NECTAR

6 Naseberries peeled and seeded
1 cup sugar

Juice of 1 orange
1 cup water

- Put all ingredients through a blender. Strain and serve chilled.

## RAIL SPLITTER

Juice of ½ lemon

2/3 jigger sugar syrup

- Pour into glass with ice and fill up with ginger beer.

# SARATOGA NO.2

Juice of ½ lemon
½ teaspoon powdered sugar

2 dash Angostura bitters
Ginger ale

- Place ingredients in tall glass with ice cubes and fill with ginger ale.

# SOURSOP PUNCH

1 ripe Soursop
4 glasses water

Condensed milk to taste
Vanilla to flavour

- Peel and crush soursop, removing seeds.
- Stir in water and strain.
- Add milk and flavouring. Serve ice cold.

# SUMMER FIZZ (FOR 8)

12 sprigs mint
½ cup lemon juice
1 cup currant jelly
1 cup hot water

1 cup cold water
3 cups orange juice
1 bottle ginger ale

- Crush mint in a bowl and add boiling water and 1 cup currant jelly.
- When jelly is melted, add cold water. Strain, when cold, into punch bowl.
- Add fruit juices and block of ice. Just before serving, pour in ginger ale and decorate with mint.

# TEETOTALLERS PUNCH (APPROX. 20 DRINKS)

½ (13 ozs.) bottle kola
3 oz. lemon juice
10 dash Angostura bitters

26 oz. dry ginger ale
26 oz. lemonade
Lemon slices

- Mix all ingredients with cracked ice in punch bowl.
- Add lemon slices and serve.

## UNLUCKY BULLY

*There's a man sitting at a bar in Ocho Rios just looking at his drink. He stays like that for half an hour. Then, a tall, well-built, trouble-making truck driver steps next to him, takes the drink from the guy, and just drinks it all down.*

*The poor man starts crying. The truck driver says, "Come on man, I was just joking. Here, I'll buy you another drink. I just can't stand to see a grown man cry."*

*"No, it's not that. This day is the worst of my life. First, I fall asleep, and I'm late to my office. My boss, in an outrage, fires me. When I leave the building to my car, I found out it was stolen. The police say they can do nothing. I get a cab to return home and when I leave it, I remember I left my wallet and credit cards there. The cab driver just drives away. I go home and when I get there, I find my wife sleeping with the gardener. I leave home and come to this bar. And when I was thinking about putting an end to my life, you show up and drink my poison."*

# Pick-Me Ups

## (Or 'The Morning After')

*Ring down the curtain, the farce is over!*

*Francojs Rabefajs*

# CORPSE REVIVER

- Shake together I part brandy I part Fernet Branca and I part White Créme de Menthe.

# HOT-BUTTERED RUM (12 SERVINGS)

8 lbs. butter.

I teaspoon nutmeg

I cup honey

10 lbs. brown sugar

I teaspoon ground cinnamon

A tiny pinch of ground cloves.

½ lb. unsalted butter, softened to room temperature and cut into pieces.

- 1/3 cup brown sugar for each individual serving.
- Add I to I¼ oz. rum, hot water to taste and a large spoonful of the butter.
- To prepare the batter, place ingredients in a large bowl, using a wooden spoon or an electric mixer, cream the butter with brown sugar, nutmeg, cinnamon, cloves and honey. Continue to beat the mixture until the mixture is completely blended and fluffy. The batter will keep, if refrigerated, for several days. When serving pour the rum into 8 oz. porcelain coffee mugs; fill the mugs with very hot water, top with a large spoonful of batter and serve.

# IRISH COFFEE

In a 6 oz. glass pour:

¾ oz. Irish Whisky

2 cubes sugar

Hot Coffee

- Heavy cream whipped until stiff with sugar to taste.
- Pour the whisky into the glass over 2 cubes of sugar, then pour the coffee down the back of metal spoon; set into the glass (to prevent cracking) remove spoon and top with whipped cream.

# PICK-ME-UP LICK-ME-DOWN COCKTAIL

- I part cognac with I part dry vermouth and I part Pastis.

# PRAIRIE OYSTER NO. 1

I jigger brandy

I dash Worcestershire Sauce

I egg

Salt if desired

- Carefully break egg into 6 oz. glass.
- Add Worcestershire Sauce and brandy.
- Blend lightly with egg white, keeping yolk intact. For the morning after.

A Caribbean vacation does not last forever and one will have to face those December months when the mood calls for elegant drink recipes to impart the warmth of a Caribbean sunshine. During my frequent battles with the cold climes I have always found these cocktails my life savers.

# Jimmy Buffett's MARGARITAVILLE®

## CARIBBEAN
### JAMAICA • GRAND CAYMAN • GRAND TURK

# OFF TO SEE THE Lizard Margarita

## Ingredients

1¼ Margaritaville Gold Tequila, 1/8 Triple Sec, 1/8 Midori (Melon Liquer), 4 oz sour mix

Shake all ingredients together with ice and serve in margarita glass. Garnish with a lime cartwheel.

# JAMMIN' REGGAE SHOT

## REDGREENANDGOLD

RED- GRENADINE
GREEN- CREME DE MENTHE
GOLD- MANGO WITH OVERPROOF WHITE RUM

# *Famous Jamaican Bars & Watering Holes*

## Jimmy Buffett's Margaritaville...

Montego Bay, Negril and Ocho Rios, all located in Jamaica have now become home to Jimmy Buffett's Margaritaville which serves as the ideal vacation location for any fun loving individual.

Margaritaville, Montego Bay is located on the "Hip Strip" on Gloucester Avenue, Montego Bay. It was opened in January 1996 by Brian Jardim and Ian Dear and caters for both the enthusiastic foreigner who wishes to embrace our culture and local Jamaicans who just want to have a good time.

Later that same year, Margaritaville Negril was opened on Negril's 7 mile stretch of beautiful white sand. However, it would be much later before Margaritaville Ocho Rios was opened in February, 2002, and it is the largest local Margaritaville, standing on 12,000 square feet. They expanded the brand to Sangsters International Airport in April of 2001 and eventually added another Air Margaritaville in December, 2006.

### LIZARD MARGARITA

| | |
|---|---|
| 1 ¼ Margaritaville's Gold Tequila | 1/8 Triple Sec |
| 1/8 Midori (Melon Liqueur) | 4 oz. Lemon X |

- Shake all ingredients together with ice and serve in margarita glass.
- Garnish with a lime and cartwheel.

### JAMMIN REGGAE SHOT – RED, GREEN AND GOLD

Red – Grenadine
Green – Cremdimint
Gold – Mango with Overproof White Rum

MISTY MOUNTAIN COFFEE RUM (page 123)

# Strawberry Hill Hotel and Spa...

This is one of the most relaxing and peaceful vacation spots in the beautiful isle of Jamaica. Located on 26 acres of land in Irish Town, 3,100 feet high in the mountains, the resort offers for you all the comfort and luxuries within one of its twelve Georgian-style cottages, its gorgeous botanical gardens housing approximately 300 species of flowers, the breathtaking backdrop of the Blue Mountain and the magnificent and sensuous scenery of the city of Kingston.

## MISTY MOUNTAIN COFFEE RUM

1 oz. Appleton Special Reserve Rum         1 oz. Tia Maria
Dash of Lime Juice                        Sprig of mint

- Fill shaker with ice and add the rum, Tia Maria and lime juice.
- Add mint leaves and shake ingredients well to infuse the mint.
- Pour over ice in glass and garnish with fresh mint and lime.

# Christophers Jazz Café...

Located off Knutsford Boulevard in New Kingston, Jamaica's "Hip Strip", Christophers Jazz Café was opened in December, 2003, by Christopher Cargill and Brian Chung. It caters to the music lover who is treated to the performances of live bands playing on Tuesday nights, as well as singers' night every Thursday. It's the ideal environment with its delicious drinks and scrumptious food, all offered against a backdrop of soulful music.

## CHRISTINI

1 oz. vodka
½ oz. lime juice
Splash of Sprite or 7 Up

½ oz. Blue Curacao
½ oz. clear syrup

• Shake and serve in martini glass.

## ISLAND BREEZE

1 oz. pina colada
½ oz. milk or cream
1 oz. coconut cream

½ oz. Blue Curacao
½ oz clear syrup

• Blend all ingredients and top with whip cream. Serve in an old fashioned glass.

## WILD TEMPTATION

1 ½ oz. Appleton V/X
½ oz. clear syrup

1 oz. peach schnapps
Splash of lime juice

• Blend all ingredients and top with cherry. Serve in a margarita glass.

ISLAND BREEZE (page 124)

CHRISTINI (page 124)

WILD TEMPTATION (page 124)

# SuperClubs...

Founded by John Issa, thirty one years ago, SuperClubs is now one of the most popular Super Inclusive resorts worldwide. With locations spanning across the Caribbean, SuperClubs resorts caters to all, whether you are looking for a family vacation or just want to 'let loose'. With five star facilities and delightful service, you are sure to have a pleasurable stay at any SuperClubs resort.

## BREEZES KISS

1 oz Passion Fruit concentrate
2 Fresh Peeled Peach halves with the heart taken out
1 Drop Angostura Bitters

1 oz Amaretto Disaronno
½ oz Rumona

- Combine all ingredients in a blender and blend until smooth.
- Pour into 9oz stemmed glass. Garnish with lavender flower.

**BREEZES KISS** (page 126)

# Terminology

Blazers

Drinks that are set alight. For a brandy blazer put a lump of sugar, a twist of lemon peel, a twist of orange peel and a lot of brandy into a flame proof mug or tankard. Light the mixture, stir and strain.

Cobblers

Ice and sweetened long drinks with a spirit of wine base. Fine ice goes into the tumbler first followed by the ingredients with the base liquor going in last.

Collins

A refreshing long drink made with Dutch gin is called a John Collins; with Old Tom it is called a Tom Collins.

Cordials

These are sweetened aromatised spirits and are regarded as heart stimulants.

Fizzes

Spirit based long drinks with a form of sweetener; in short a sour made to fizz with soda water or other aerated waters.

Frappes

Drinks served with broken or crushed up ice (as opposed to cubes, i.e. 'on the rocks'). The ice goes in first into a long or medium glass followed by a liqueur and two straws. Créme de Menthe frappe compliments your supper on a hot summer night.

Highballs

A long iced drink consisting of a base liquid combined with carbonated beverages but without citrus juices.

Rickeys

A spirit based drink with fresh limes or other fruit if you are unable to get limes. Gin, Sloe Gin and Rum make the best rickeys.

| Smashes | Mixed iced drinks flavoured with mint. |
| Sours | Spirit based drinks with citrus fruit juice and usually a sweetener. Also called daises, crustas and fixes. |
| Toddies | Usually sweetened hot drinks. |

# *Fruits of Jamaica*

**Banana**

It is one of the most popularly consumed fruit island wide. Usually, it is cooked when green and consumed as a staple but it is eaten raw, when ripe. It is often times blended, when used in mixed drinks, which causes the drink to have a thick, creamy consistency and delicious flavour. See *Banana Daiquiri* (page 2).

**Coconut**

A nut. Its fleshy interior can be eaten and/or the water drunk. When the nut is dried the interior is blended to make coconut milk, a very important and tasty ingredient in popular Jamaican recipes such as rice and peas. It is the water that is used in the preparation of refreshing drinks. See *Coconut Oak* (page 3).

**Coffee**

Produced from coffee beans, it is one of Jamaica's most popular export fruits. Blue Mountain Coffee is world renown for its distinct taste and flavour. It can be used to make a hot beverage or as a liqueur in such recipes as *Brown Cow* (page 70).

**Grapefruit**

A citrus fruit. There are different varieties the most popular being the red, white and pink all referring to the colour of the flesh inside. All these varieties are tart in flavour; as such it helps to give mixed drinks a tangy taste. See *Grapefruit Cocktail* (page 26).

**Mango**

A tropical fruit. The flesh of this fruit is usually very sweet and is eaten raw when ripe and used to make mango chutney when half ripe. The flesh makes very refreshing fruit juice and is a basic ingredient that every bar should have.

| | |
|---|---|
| Orange | Like the grapefruit it is a citrus fruit. It is usually peeled and eaten or juiced. Its juice is a very popular chaser and is a must have for every bar. See *Orange Dawn* (page 69). |
| Passion Fruit | A small round fruit filled with numerous juicy seeds. It can be eaten when ripe or used for its juice to add aroma and flavour in drinks such as *Passion Daiquiri* (page 9). |
| Pineapple | A tropical fruit with a very prickly exterior and juicy interior. It is usually eaten raw, used in recipes such as sweet and sour chicken or can be juiced and included in drinks such as *Pineapple Cocktail* (page 11). |
| Naseberry | A small, round fruit with very smooth skin. The flesh of the fruit is very sweet and flavourful and makes a delicious drink, *Naseberry Nectar* (page 113). |
| Soursop | A spiky, green fruit with a white, pulpy interior with seeds. In Jamaica, it is usually juiced and sweetened with condensed milk and vanilla is added for flavour. See *Soursop Punch* (page 114). |
| Watermelon | A large fruit with a smooth exterior. Its interior has multiple small seeds but the fruit is juicy and refreshing when eaten; as such it is a suitable ingredient to be included in mixed drinks such as *Watermelon Martini* (page 15). |

# Your Liquor Reference

Amaretto | Italy's delicious almond flavoured liqueur.

Angostura | Bitters made from various herbs and spices, which can be added to food and drinks.

Anisette 44° | Sweetened version of Anis, makes a long drink with bitter lemon, ice and a little lime juice.

Aperitif | A drink taken to stimulate one's appetite, usually a wine based cocktail.

Apricot Brandy 42° | A highly flavoured liqueur made from apricots.

Beer | The name for five types of fermented malt beverages: Lager Beer, the most popular type of light; Dry Beer; Ale, having a more pronounced flavour and aroma of hops. It is heavier, more bitter than lager beer and stout.

Benedictine 73° | A sweet herb flavoured brandy based liquor. One of the oldest liqueurs in the world and originally made by The Benedictine Monks. Can be mixed with equal parts of brandy and is sometimes referred to as D.O.M.

Bitters | A blend of roots and herbs used for flavouring. Best known brands are Angostura, Ferr Branca and Peychauds.

Brandy | Distilled from fermented juice of nice grapes and other fruits. The best of the brandies being cognac.

Calvados | A french apple brandy.

| | |
|---|---|
| Cherry Brandy 42° | A brandy based in the juices of ripe cherries. |
| Coconut Milk | Made from the juice of coconut. |
| Cointreau 70° | A sweet colourless liqueur with orange flavour. |
| Coconut Rum | Based on the juice of the coconut and fine spirits. |
| Coconut Liqueur | A delightful liqueur made from the juice of the coconut and blended with spirits. |
| Créme de Banana 42° | A yellow brandy based liqueur flavoured with bananas. |
| Créme de Cacao 42° | A very sweet dark liqueur made from cacao beans, vanilla and spices. |
| Crème de Cassis | A liqueur with black currant flavour. |
| Créme de Menthe | A peppermint flavoured liqueur in green, white or red. |
| Dubonnet | A dark red French aperitif wine with red wine base and a slight quinine taste. |
| Galliano 70° | A gold flavoured liqueur with liquorice and anisette flavour. |
| Gin | Alcohol made from any source of sugar. Tasteless until re-distilled with juniper berries, coriander seeds, angelica roots, calemus, cardamom seeds and orris powder to name the principal flavouring ingredients. |
| Grand Marnier | French brandy liqueur with orange flavour; brown in colour. |
| Grenadine | Red artificial flavouring used for sweeteners. |
| Green Ginger Wine | Wine made from fruit and Jamaican ginger. |
| Lillet | A French aperitif with white wine base. |
| Magnum | Tonic wine made from various herbs, produced by J.Wray and Nephew in Jamaica. |

| | |
|---|---|
| Mango Juice | Juice made from the mango fruit. |
| Maraschino 45° | A colourless cherry flavoured liqueur from Italy and Yugoslavia. |
| Midori | Melon liqueur. |
| Orange Bitters 70° | Made from the peel swilles bitter oranges; much used in flavourings. |
| Papaya Juice/Syrup | Made from the juice of the papaya fruit. |
| Peach Brandy 45° | A brandy coloured liqueur with peach flavour. |
| Pimento Liqueur | A liqueur made from the pimento plant which is only to be found in Jamaica; a sharp biting taste. |
| Red Bull | Popular energy drink that is commonly consumed on the Jamaican party scene. |
| Schnapps 66.5° | Scandinavian liqueur made from potatoes and flavoured with caraway seeds. |
| Sorrel | Fruit that is used to make a traditional Christmas drink, with the addition of ginger and rum, in Jamaica. |
| Triple Sec | White Curacao. A colourless liqueur with a sweet orange flavour. |
| Tequila 66.5° | A Mexican drink made from Pulque – a beverage from the cactus plant also called century plant, agave, mescal. The Mexican way to drink this brew is 'a lick of salt from the back of the hand and a sip of the tequila.' |
| Vodka | An alcoholic distillate from a fermented mash of grain; it is odourless and colourless. |
| Whisky | A spirit obtained from distillation of a fermented mash of grain i.e. barley, maize and rice mainly and aged in wood. |

# Index